# SPIRIT DRIVEN SUCCESS

# DANI JOHNSON

**DESTINY IMAGE® PUBLISHERS, INC.**

P.O. Box 310, Shippensburg, PA 17257-0310

*"Speaking to the Purposes of God for This Generation and for the Generations to Come."*

This book and all other Destiny Image, Revival Press, MercyPlace, Fresh Bread, Destiny Image Fiction, and Treasure House books are available at Christian bookstores and distributors worldwide.

For a U.S. bookstore nearest you, call 1-800-722-6774.

For more information on foreign distributors, call 717-532-3040.

Or reach us on the Internet: www.destinyimage.com.

ISBN 10: 0-7684-3119-0
ISBN 13: 978-0-7684-3119-3
Previous ISBN: 0-9789551-2-0

For Worldwide Distribution, Printed in the U.S.A.

7 8 9 10 11 / 14 15 16 17 18

# SPIRIT DRIVEN SUCCESS

Father in Heaven, in the name of Jesus, I dedicate this book to You. Have Your way with it.

To Kristina, Arika, Cabe, Roman, and Micah. May you never limit the limitless God. Set the world on fire with your passion for Him.

## ACKNOWLEDGMENTS

First, thank You Jesus Christ for saving my soul—for being my Strong Tower. Truly *I am nothing without You.* Thank You for allowing me to do this and for bringing the hands to help. All glory is Yours.

To the most amazing husband on the planet, Hans—you have powerfully used your gifts to push our message out into the marketplace. I love you more than words can say.

To all five of my babies—you support me and believe in *our* calling. You are the best a mom could ever ask for. If you weren't who you are, I couldn't do what I do. I love you sooo much!

To Marla Fairfield—you attacked this project and pressed through obstacles to bring it to pass. The hoops you jumped through were insane. Thanks for doing whatever it took to get this done.

To Holly McClure—you showed up out of nowhere and shocked us with the precious gift of making this happen. Thanks for the all-nighters by the fire. Thanks for pressing through when others said that it was impossible to get done.

To Jack and Lavonne—you allowed God to use you to save our marriage years ago. If Hans and I weren't together, this ministry would not be happening. Your wise counsel is priceless, and you taught me how to stand on the true Word of God. Thank you for your unconditional love, belief, encouragement, and support.

To Ruthie Brown—you taught me how to fight in the spirit realm and how to not back down; you taught me how to pray. Thank you for loving me unconditionally through a lot of my immaturity through the years. I am forever grateful to you.

To JP—Dude...look at this! You saw something in a 19-year-old kid that she couldn't see herself. Thanks for always believing in me even when I didn't believe in myself.

To Ed Negrelli—you planted the first seed in me when I was young and stupid, unbelieving, untrained, and ignorant. Thank you! You were the first one to get me to think bigger than me. Look how God used you to touch one life who has touched hundreds of thousands of lives. I am forever grateful for you.

To Mona McGrady—you have been our advocate! Thank you for the 2 a.m. to 4 a.m. night watch and for your years of dedication to the vision. Can you believe God lets us do this?

To Jeribai Tascoe—you have done a phenomenal job on everything you touch. Your gift in design is outrageous. You have been a huge blessing to our team.

To our team of intercessors—look what God has done! Your prayers are fruitful. Thank you for your years of service and your commitment to the call.

To the entire DJC team—Brian, Marla, Gerri, Mona, Joseph, Jenn, Tim, JP, Ed, Jeribai, Isa, Ryan, Nina, LauraLee, Andrew, Arika, Diana, Judi, Robyn, Elyssa, Tammy, Jordan, Gabe, Jeremy, Patrick, Laurie, Kim, Penny, and Juana. Wow!

I could write another book on you alone! Thank you for your dedication, commitment, persistence, and tenacity. Thank you for applying what you have learned and for reaching higher. Thank you for all the hands that have touched this project in one way or another. Thank you for your love for Him.

To our clients—you are our friends; you are amazing! Thank you for running with this teaching, embracing it, and attacking the marketplace with it. You have produced results that have caught the attention of nations. This adventure would be useless to me without you.

To Mom—thank you for not aborting me. Look what God has done. I love you.

to hear God's voice and follow His direction by helping me understand what His Word says about life, love, business, parenting, everything! Her practical and honest style has taught me victory through Jesus in every area of my life. If you want more confidence and direction in your life, don't wait another minute, start today.

—Tracy S

Thank you so much for all that you do to minister life and healing in the area of personal development and wealth to hundreds of thousands, if not millions, of people around the world. One of the things I admire most about you is the fact that you give glory and honor to God the Father and the Lord Jesus Christ in everything that you do. I was thrilled and exhilarated when I attended First Steps Spiritual Equipping and had the freedom to worship and praise Him. As a believer, I feel safe submitting myself to your training and referring my friends, family, and associates to you as well.

—Jennifer R

The Lord inspired me in your message. My business has exploded!

—Chris W

My life is on *fire*! Not only has your program ignited my business, but it has affected every area of my life! Communicating with others has always been easy for me, yet after your training I find myself interfacing with others in a completely different way. What a gift!

—Cynthia K

I praise God for you! Not only am I learning business strategies, but also my entire life is changing, and everyone around me notices! I love you!

—Michelle A

I'm so blessed that God brought me to you! I was listening for a change! I got *financial freedom*!

—Karen U

Prior to Dani's training I spent so much time working and didn't want to hear anything my husband had to say to me because I thought that I was the "bread winner" of the house. I thought I was coming to Dani to learn how to grow my business, but I had a new revelation. I realized God had chosen my husband for me and that he was the king in my life and I had to lift him up. I learned how to balance my life and within days, my whole life started to change.

—LaShonda C

I had achieved a six-figure income but I was absolutely miserable. I had no time freedom, I didn't see my children, and was losing control of my life. After coming to Dani Johnson, I've learned so many skills to gain manageability of my own life and business. It's improved my marriage. I now earn a multiple six-figure income and paid off over $100,000 worth of debt. I haven't seen one person who hasn't been phenomenally affected by the training, equipping, and the personal growth that occurs with Dani Johnson.

—Renae H

Before meeting Dani Johnson, I had spent close to $100,000 on personal growth seminars and workshops, only to find myself living from paycheck to paycheck, renting a room in someone else's home, and dealing with bad relationships. Since training with Dani, I have never had to interview for any positions I have held—employers recruited me! If you know people who need help with people skills, encouragement, or a new direction in life, they need to discover the Dani Johnson system now.

—Dawn L

Being able to plug into Spirit-Driven Success, I've learned so many things that have set me free. It's allowed me to raise my children up for success instead of bondage. It's allowed me to completely restore and heal my marriage. This is something that is going to completely equip you and teach you to open up your heart and receive all of that and to allow Him to work in your life and to start living in peace instead of constant resistance.

—ANONYMOUS

# CONTENTS

*You are the light of the world. A city on a hill cannot be hidden...Let your light shine before men, that they may see your good deeds and praise your Father in heaven* (Matthew 5:14,16).

Does success consist of more than driving fancy cars, living in a big house, dropping important names at cocktail parties, and taking exotic vacations? Is there more to life than volunteering for yet another church program while you struggle to pay your bills and make ends meet?

Are we really being told the complete truth about what success is and what success is not by our society, our media, and our churches? Does the Church's traditional definition of success measure up to God's biblical definition of success? Is it really possible to achieve your dreams, yet still do the work of your Father in Heaven?

In *Spirit-Driven Success*, Dani Johnson answers all of these questions and more. However, she doesn't stop there. Dani shows you specific changes that you need to make in order to start experiencing immediate results in every area of your life.

*Spirit-Driven Success* offers a radical new approach to a subject as old as time. It is a message that is long overdue, and it has already changed the lives of countless people who have attended Dani's live seminars and events.

As a successful businesswoman, mega-entrepreneur, mother of five, and loving wife, Dani is the real deal, through and through. She lives and breathes what she teaches. I know this because, as both her husband and her lifelong business partner, I've personally witnessed her heart and character behind the scenes in our business, personal, and family life. I can tell you that her integrity, sincerity, and desire to equip others to succeed is surpassed only by her passion to serve God.

In *Spirit-Driven Success*, Dani will share in her raw, candid, straight-from-the-gut style the biblical success secrets that she has discovered and applied in her own life. These truths enabled her to go from being homeless to making millions to becoming one of the most sought-after business coaches in the world today.

The concepts in *Spirit-Driven Success* have shown tens of thousands of others how to improve their lives spiritually, mentally, emotionally, physically, and financially. Will you be next?

Why do you have this book in your hands? Are you looking for change? Are you looking for financial independence? Do you want to take your career or business to new levels of growth, prosperity, and success? Do you want to create a legacy for your family that lasts generations?

This book will show you *how* to do it so that your Father in Heaven may be glorified.

—HANS JOHNSON

## INTRODUCTION

I grew up in a home filled with daily verbal and physical abuse from a drug-addicted stepfather who was pathetically enabled by my indifferent, drug-addicted mother. My two sisters and I were often the targets of my stepfather's violent temper in a home where constant emotional turmoil, verbal assaults, physical beatings, and even sexual abuse were daily events throughout my childhood and teenage years.

While still in my teens, I escaped my psychotic home life and began working a number of short-term jobs, but never really excelled at anything. No matter what I attempted to do, every day I would hear the constant barrage of my stepfather's criticism ringing in my ears, "You're fat. You're ugly. And you're good for nothing!"

In my search to prove him wrong, and prove to myself that I could break free from the bondage of his curses, I decided to become an entrepreneur. Within a few months, with only the education of hard knocks, I failed miserably. I realized that I needed knowledge, skills, and intensive training to equip my determination. Although I could not afford it at the time, I decided to invest in some business training classes. It was the best money I ever spent; for the first time in my life, I had invested in me!

Within six months, I became one of the top sales leaders in my company, enjoying all of the income and praise that comes with being a young top producer. I likewise gained the confidence I needed to succeed in a highly competitive business world. I was treated like a celebrity, had plenty of money, and was sought out by people who wanted to learn from me. *From me!* The "fat, ugly, good for nothing" entrepreneur was on a mission to prove her stepfather wrong.

While I was at a training event, one of the attendees came over and asked me if he could "pick my brain" for some business tips. He was movie-star handsome, he was incredibly charming, and he made me feel wanted, appreciated, and important. We fell head-over-heels in love, spent a romantic and passionate week together, and married in a romantic whirlwind. I was convinced I had finally found my "happily ever after" perfect life.

But within four months, my handsome husband left me for another woman, took all of my money, and left me with a $35,000 debt and exactly $2.03 to my name. At that same time, my business was embezzled by a man who had actually taught me a few things about building my business. I was devastated, abandoned, confused, alone, and very scared.

Everything I owned was packed into my tiny car. I lived at public beaches, slept in my car, showered in public facilities, and tried to sort through the devastation I felt over losing everything: my husband, my business, my savings, my friends, my dignity, and worst of all, my dreams. I had lost all hope, and I had no vision for the future. I had become the awful words that my stepfather had spoken over me.

I managed to get a job as a cocktail waitress and spent most of my days smoking pot with friends and working afternoon shifts. It was Christmas time, and at a work party, I did something I swore I would never do. I was offered a line of cocaine, and I took it! The next day, I found myself on a beach, desperate for another line of cocaine, for anything that would numb the pain of my existence and make me forget my horrendous life.

While people were partying on the beach, I got up and walked into the ocean. As I waded out to the waves, I dove under one that was about to break, and when I stood up, I heard the words: "Pick up your mat and walk." I instantly went to my beach towel, picked it up, and left. As I drove down the highway, I realized that a change had come over me. The drugged and foggy feeling was gone, and the craving for cocaine was gone. Moments before, I had been gripped by an overpowering urge to get more drugs, but now that desperation was completely *gone*. Gone were the angry thoughts, the depression, the despair, the hopelessness.

I did not question the voice because I knew it was God. And I heard the words, "God did not intend for you to be mediocre and average; this life you're living is not for you."

The next day I started a business from the trunk of my car and a pay phone booth. I was completely focused: no more whining, crying the blues, complaining, or pity parties. Within a couple days I made $2000, and within my first year of business I made a quarter of a million dollars. By the second year, I made my first million. All by the age of 23! Since then, I have made millions and millions of dollars building businesses and helping other people to succeed financially.

I have had outrageous success as well as devastating hardships—life is not perfect just because you believe in God. With every step, God has been in every circumstance of my life. I am blown away by His incredible love. I marvel at each experience that God has both blessed me with and brought me through. Each experience has made me who I am today.

God's love is, and has always been, constant. How precious and forgiving is the God I turned my back on years ago. Even through my hurt, rejection, and anger at life, He was the Father I never had, who loved me, disciplined me, and welcomed me, His prodigal daughter, home.

My life is much more than I ever dreamed possible. Blessed with a loving husband, five wonderful children, an amazing circle of friends, and an incredible staff, I am in awe of my success as a speaker, business trainer, and spiritual success coach, and I am eternally grateful for my amazing clients all over the world.

I do not take where I am in life for granted. My success is not because of anything I did or deserve to have, but entirely because of God's grace, mercy, and favor over my life. I have practiced the principles of this book, and, simply put, they work. I am reaping what I have sown. How grateful I am for God's deliverance from a life that was doomed by man's words—but redeemed by the Word of God.

—DANI JOHNSON

*Until I listened to your training, I thought I was going*
*to have to choose between having a spiritual life and*
*having a business. Hearing how you have been able*
*to balance between the two has given me hope.*

—FRAN W

CHAPTER I

# SPIRIT-DRIVEN SUCCESS

If there is one lesson in life that I have learned, it is this: You never know when your life is about to change. You never know when one decision will dramatically impact your life and change the course of your destiny. Are you standing at the crossroads in your life?

As I travel around the world doing training seminars and coaching business clients, I am truly amazed at the number of people who tell me they are standing at a crossroads. Most of them are searching for something in their lives that seems to be missing, something that lets them know they make a difference in this world.

While the people I meet around the world have present situations and personal stories that differ in many ways, they all appear to have one thing in common—they have lost their dream and vision for what they were created to do.

Too many people in our society have settled for mediocrity. For one reason or another, their lives have been put on cruise control, and with each passing day, their feelings of emptiness grow. Maybe this is where you are at right now, standing at the crossroads of life. If this sounds like you, if you can relate to what I am saying, I have an important message for you that will change your life.

My words are simple. Don't you dare put your life in a box! Don't you dare decide to settle for mediocrity! Don't you dare give up on your dreams! Don't you dare give up on your life! No matter how comfortable you are, no matter how much or how little you have accomplished in life, do not ever stop dreaming. Don't just do this for yourself, but do it for the sake of your loved ones, for the sake of your spouse, and for the sake of your children.

To dare to dream in the midst of adversity, in the midst of failure, in the midst of complacency, is to have hope. That hope, that dream, is a gift from God. It is His way of telling you that He has a plan for your life if you will listen and give Him a chance to bring it to pass.

## HE DID IT FOR ME

I know because God gave me a dream, and He took it far beyond the limits I had placed on it; He magnified it far beyond anything I could have ever imagined. I grew up in an environment that had no hope, no dreams, no faith in what I could be. I only heard criticism and condemnation related to what I was expected to become. I came from an environment of verbal, emotional, and physical abuse. And my past would choke any dreams or hopes I tried to have, and it would label me with a life doomed for failure.

I look at the kind of mom I am today and I thank God that my home is the absolute opposite of the home in which I was raised. My God rescued me from my past, blessed me with an awesome family, and surrounded me with great people, great clients, and great friends who have all made a massive impact on my life. I believe with all my heart that each one of us has been given unique gifts from our Creator and that each of us is called to apply those gifts to a purpose in life.

In order for you to understand the principles of this book and what I want to teach you, you must understand where I came from so that you will realize what I can do for you.

I hope you read the Introduction because in it I explain my beginnings and the background I came from. If you're like me, you probably skip the Introduction and go straight to the good stuff, but please, go back and read my story so that you can appreciate what I'm about to share with you. It will help you understand why the principles in this book will radically change your life.

## FINDING SUCCESS IN LIFE

Through our businesses we have helped tens of thousands of people all over the world improve their lifestyles and finances. I have seen people healed emotionally, physically, spiritually, and financially. I have seen them get out of debt, become financially independent, and even become millionaires.

Are you struggling financially, physically, mentally, emotionally, socially, or relationally? Are you trying to find your purpose and place in God's Kingdom? If you are nodding your head in agreement, then please pay close attention to this book. Together we will explore how others have walked down this path and triumphed.

Is there an area of dissatisfaction in your life? Is something in your life not quite right? I'm talking about your life. I'm not just talking about your career or your business. Are you fully satisfied in your marriage? Are you fully satisfied as a parent? Are you fully satisfied as a leader in your community? Are you fully satisfied as a son or daughter of the Most High God? If you aren't, don't give up. Don't stay in a rut. Don't keep the status quo.

Since 2003, I have helped thousands to wildly succeed in the marketplace and achieve financial freedom. In these very same "business" seminars, where key principles of debt and finances are taught, I have also seen God's hand touch lives and change them forever.

I've seen miracle after miracle with documented testimonies. Here are just a couple of the lives that have changed:

- Krisztina and Andy, who had lived together for 12 years, came to First Steps to Success and got saved during the weekend. Since then, they have gotten married, have quadrupled their income, and just bought their first property.

- Carman from Michigan came to one of my business seminars and, after learning key principles and business skills, went from making $700,000 a year to $3.7 million in just 18 months. She turned her life and business over to the Lord. She was radically moved by the Most High God. And she risked her business reputation and her relationship with her employees and customers by now boldly professing Christ in the marketplace. She could have lost it all and been labeled as a Jesus freak, but God continues to bless her.

- Douglas from Georgia came to a two-day business seminar, and during the Spiritual Equipping Session, he and his wife watched his leg grow four inches! They both became believers that night and are raising their children in His way.

Not only have I had the privilege and honor of helping my clients make millions of dollars, I have also seen God's anointing on our seminars in the following ways:

- Healing of marriages

- Paying off of millions of dollars of debt

- Grooming of children for success

- Release from all kinds of bondage

- Restoration of families

- Quadrupling of businesses

- And so much more

I have seen the Spirit of God move in amazing ways. God planted the desire in me to equip the saints to succeed so that the world would not control His people. I love Isaiah 61; it is my life Scripture. It talks about releasing the captives and bringing the prisoners light and freedom.

## THE PATH TO FREEDOM

Have you walked away from God? Have people let you down? I could spend hours telling you what the Lord has done for me and how He brought me out of a condemned lifestyle and set me on a path to free others. I pray He reveals to you what His power is about, what His grace is, and what His blessing is for you.

So I ask this again: Are you satisfied financially, physically, mentally, emotionally, socially, and relationally?

If you can't say yes to all of these, don't give up. Don't stay in a rut. Don't keep the status quo. God did not intend those areas of your life to be mediocre. Don't choose to live under your own excuses. I learned that it is never our circumstances that defeat us; it is how we choose to deal with the circumstances that determines the outcome of our lives.

You may not realize it, but skill, talent, and ability are sitting dormant in you, waiting to come out. If you are genuinely seeking to release these gifts, I want to give you a shortcut, a direct path to rediscover and awaken those gifts that have been buried inside you.

In this book, I can only point you toward the source that guided me through some incredibly difficult times. This source is the only One who was able to penetrate my heart, start me on a new path, and bring me to where I am today. And believe me, I know. I've tried many different and misdirected ways to get at the truth.

The last thing I want to come across as is a Bible-thumping fanatic who wants to shove Scripture down everyone's throat. However, I do want to tell you the truth about what happened to me and how the God who is revealed in Scripture has been faithful to all His promises.

Because of the transformations that I have seen in my own life and in the lives of my clients, I believe that the Bible is the greatest success book ever written. It is jam-packed full of wisdom, insights, and messages—God's direct communications with us.

I have read the Bible from cover to cover several times, and each time I am blown away by the treasures that are hidden in the stories, the situations, the characters, the psalms, the proverbs, and the parables. Although each story in the Bible contains some obvious lessons, the real treasures are sometimes buried a little bit deeper.

My hope is that you will discover the mentor, coach, encourager, and loving Father God who knows your heart and wants to satisfy your every need. Since I began my relationship with my Lord and Savior, He has healed my heart and set me free to live a life bigger than I could have ever asked for or imagined.

If you are one of those searching to reclaim that true vision for your life, then it is time for you to find your path, uncover your true gifts, and step forward into the journey that God has planned for you.

It is time to turn your back on the life you lived before. It is time to turn your back on the things that have been holding you back. Set your sights on achieving a success wilder than you can even imagine, and choose a path of higher calling—the path God intended for you.

Start living your life with *Spirit-driven success.*

*I was a doubter, but now I have no other choice but to believe and lead others! Dani and her "folks" have lived what they are teaching!*

—Thomas A

CHAPTER 2

# LIES WE'VE LEARNED

My life is a living testimony of what I am sharing with you. I have found a God who has given me everything that I have, and it has been for a unique purpose that is completely different than anything I would've ever imagined. It's much bigger than I ever thought it would be.

Why was I a broke, homeless cocktail waitress who became a millionaire in two years? It was at least in part so that you'd pick up this book and get this message. If I was still broke, you wouldn't read this book.

God has put a calling on your life, but unfortunately, the picture that's been painted for you is separate from the picture that God has painted for you. You're a piece in a very big picture—a picture that will change the world for God's glory. You are a dynamic member of the Body of Christ. Do you believe it? Are you living like it?

According to George Barna's book, *Revolution*, 80 percent of the Church is absolutely inactive. I believe it too. You might want to get a hold of his book. Barna is a well-known pollster in the United States, and in this case, the question that he asked people was, "Where do you get your influence?" It might make some of you sick to know the answers. (I'll discuss this in a later chapter.)

In much of the Church there's a big disconnect. Sunday we do our little church thing; we act like a good ole Christian boy or girl, and on Monday we go do a different thing. Then we come back on Sunday and repent for the different things that we did Monday through Saturday. So we are taught this passive Christianity that gives no vision for God's calling for our lives.

Who is raising up people to succeed in the marketplace with godly principles? Who is truly shepherding the flock? Unfortunately, not many are. Instead, several lies have captivated much of the Church and kept many of us from embracing our part in the big picture. Let's look at those lies and then discuss the truth about every believer's call to active participation in the work of the Kingdom.

## LIE #1: THE LOTTERY GOD

The first lie is the lottery message that is being preached in many churches. They say, "Oh, well if you just sow into my ministry today, I just know, I can feel it, there's somebody out there with $1,000. Ooh, there's somebody out there with $1,000—ooh, I think there's somebody out there with $2,000. God is going to bless you if you sow into my ministry right now. Ooh, I see it. It's coming!"

We've all seen that, and some of us have even written the checks. That's a lottery message—a message that it is not much different from buying a lottery ticket. I am not saying that God won't bless you or that these preachers are not hearing from God; what I am saying, however, is there is more to receiving a blessing than being manipulated into writing a big check.

An example: Someone is continuously irresponsible financially and ridden with debt because of ignorant spending habits. His hope for becoming debt free is winning the lottery, until he hears the preacher say, "God is going to cancel your debt if you give $1,000 right now, and it's only good for tonight." The person gives and then goes home and turns on the TV and buy something from another infomercial after stopping by the grocery store to buy some late-night junk food. This is the same person who gossips about his boss and does not work with a spirit of excellence. But God is going to cancel his debt? I'm not sure about that. I believe that is chasing a fantasy, and according to my Bible, poverty is waiting for that person (see Prov. 28:19).

Let me tell you why the lottery message does not work. *It nullifies the laws of success that are written in the Bible.* You cannot sow a seed and then just sit and expect something to happen. That's against the laws of success in the Bible. That is the message that's being taught, and it infuriates me.

My Bible says ask, seek, knock (see Matt. 7:7-8). Ask. Seek. Knock. Those are action words. It doesn't say ask and sit; it says, ask, seek, knock. But so many people think, "I wrote a check, so I'm waiting for my blessing." It's the lottery message, just like when the pastor promises: "God's going to cancel your debt this year. I can feel it. God is going to cancel your debt this year."

Oh really? Who's debt is He going to cancel? According to my Bible, He is not going to cancel someone's debt if the person is completely irresponsible and continues to be irresponsible because the person will simply wind up in debt again.

According to my Bible, God gives you whatever you can be trusted with, as it says in Matthew 25, *"Well done, good and faithful servant! You have been faithful with a few things; I will put you in charge of many things. Come and share your master's happiness"* (Matt. 25:21). In this Parable of the Talents, the master praised the servants who invested his money well. The man who was given five talents earned five more, and he was rewarded for it.

That's what God is saying to us: "I'll give you five talents; you turn it into ten. You get to keep all ten. Now you go and make it happen again." That's what it says. It says that if you can be trusted with what you have, then you'll be given much. But many Christians believe in a Fantasia God. That's called idolatry the last time I checked. So what do they end up with? Hope deferred, which only makes the heart sick (see Prov. 13:12).

Here's an example. Let's say that a management position opens up in a company. In line for that management position are two people. One says he is saved and loves God. The other is a complete heathen who is addicted to pornography, full of greed, and spends his time drinking and partying.

The guy who's addicted to pornography is absolutely diligent and hardworking and does whatever it takes to get a promotion. But the one who calls himself a Christian, who has heard the lottery message, hears about the management position and says, "Well, I'm just going to pray about it." He prays about it, but does nothing to increase his skills to ensure that he will get that promotion. He does nothing to co-labor with Christ other than chase a fantasy that says, "Well, I'm a child of God, and He loves me, so that position is mine." Not if you can't do the work.

As Jesus said in the Parable of the Talents, God gives to each of us according to our ability (see Matt. 25:15). You have the power to increase your ability. You do not have to settle for what you have now. The Bible says that if you're diligent with what you have, then God will give you more.

Certainly this is not possible on your own strength. You're stupid if you try to do it all on your own. If you're smart, you will ask an infinite, supernatural God to give you supernatural strategies, abilities, and favor with people in the marketplace. Ask Him for supernatural prophetic gifting so that you can know things about people that you normally would not know, which will enable you to speak into their lives.

## LIE #2: THE POVERTY GOD

This lie is the opposite of the last, but it, too, produces passivity, crippling many believers who would otherwise be very successful in the marketplace. This lie says that in order to be meek, you must be broke. But there's not one place in my Bible where it says that. There's not one. Meekness is a condition of the heart, not a condition of your bank account. I have searched, and if you need to know, you go search yourself. I have searched that thing high and low, studied it over and over again (see Prov. 6:9-11; 14:23; 21:5; 28:22). Poverty is a choice. It's your choice. Are you going to follow the laws to succeed, or are you going to follow the laws to fail?

There are keys to poverty and there are keys to wealth, and they both come from the same God. Unfortunately, only one side is preached, only one message is given, and the message in most places is this: "Whooo, you better watch out, because it's much easier for a camel to get through an eye of a needle than it is for a rich man to get to Heaven. Money is the root of all evil—be careful; don't get all caught up in that materialism."

## LIE #3: THE PERFECTIONIST GOD

The third lie is not about money, but it also keeps people from living out their calling to succeed by telling them they're not good enough for God to use them. I spent many years of my life feeling this way. I had such a horrible R-rated past with countless mistakes. I felt that I would never be good enough, righteous enough, pure enough, or holy enough for God to use me. This was all a plan from the pit of hell to keep me doing anything in the Kingdom of God and being completely useless.

So many are preaching the message, "You have to be holy. You have to be righteous." I believe the heart is right, but I think the method is wrong. People have preached that message as though holiness is something that you attain through things that you do or don't do. That takes God out of the picture. That is idolatry.

It's the same with righteousness. It is taught as though you can gain righteousness based on your actions. But the last time I checked my Bible, Abraham, who was a sinner, was called righteous, not based on his actions, but on his faith in God (see Rom. 4:9).

Holiness is a direct result of submitting 100 percent of your life to God. It is the fruit that comes out of you as a direct result of submitting your life to Him. It is not based on what you wear; it is not based on what you drink or what you eat. Holiness and righteousness come forth by the spirit of the living, holy, righteous God. Man can't produce holiness or righteousness. It is not humanly possible.

It is only possible when we live out John 15, where Jesus says, *"I am the vine; you are the branches. If a man remains in Me and I in him, he will bear much fruit; apart from Me you can do nothing"* (John 15:5). An apple tree naturally produces apples with no striving. The buds naturally grow into apples because they remain connected to the vine (or in that case, the tree).

Have you tried to become holy on your own? You only become holy and righteous by remaining in Christ. Through His grace, mercy, and unconditional love, He begins to produce righteousness within you. It is the fruit of who He is in you, and it is not based on what you wear or don't wear, whether you speak perfectly, what you eat or drink, and so forth. It's based on being with Him.

Are you tired of trying to become holy enough to be used by God? He loves you, and He's going to use you the way He used the disciples. After all of the disciples failed Christ (see Matt. 26:56), after Peter denied Him (see Luke 22:54-62), after Thomas asked for proof (see John 20:25), Jesus still commissioned them to begin His Church. He said, *"Go into all the world and preach the good news to all creation"* (Mark 16:15). He commissioned them to heal the sick, cleanse the lepers, raise the dead, and set the captives free by saying, *"As the Father has sent Me, I am sending you"* (John 20:21). He called His disciples to share the Gospel with the world after they messed up, after they proved themselves unholy, unrighteous, and impure. They hadn't even gone to seminary, but Jesus chose them and made them holy through His grace.

The gifts of the Spirit have also been taught as though they only exist within the four walls of the church, as though they are reserved for the super-spiritual. But that's not in my Bible. And it doesn't say that the gifts of the Spirit are only for those who have gone to seminary. It doesn't even say that the gifts of the Spirit are only for those who are pure and holy and righteous according to man's standards. It doesn't say that. It says that God has given them to all believers (see 1 Cor. 12:4-6).

## THE TRUTH

Many of us have believed one or all of these lies. We've believed that receiving a blessing from God is like the lottery. Or we've believed that poverty was holier than wealth. Or we've believed we're not holy enough to really be used for God's Kingdom. I was so deceived, but not by any man. I was deceived by the devil. But now I know the truth.

The truth is, your Daddy loves you. He loves the way He made you, and He made you for a unique and strategic perfect position. He made you for something specific. He made you to actively participate in a very big picture. And you don't have to be perfect before you can do it.

We cannot keep trying to fit into a box, whether the box is Christian or not. Perhaps your box comes from another religion, or maybe your box is just business and you believe, "I don't get to serve God because I'm not holy enough." The point is, it's not about a box. It's about relationship.

And relationship is about honor. I am a child of God. He is my Daddy. And He is pleased when I honor Him by tithing from my income, by showing myself trustworthy with what I've been given, and by being diligent and hardworking when I honor people and live by His commandments of loving Him and my neighbor. When I show myself faithful, I am serving my Master.

Yes, God wants to extravagantly bless His children. He wants Daddy's girls and boys to get the promotion. But I won't get that position if I am not doing my part. The lottery message is, ask and sit. But the truth is, as children, we must honor our Father with our hard work and faithfulness so that He can bless us with more responsibility. They can't be separated.

The truth is also that being diligent and hardworking and faithful does not mean you have to be perfect. We're in process. The important thing is that we're becoming more faithful instead of sitting on our butts and waiting for a lottery blessing.

I truly believe that if there are two contractors bidding on a job, the one who serves the Most High God and who is diligent and works with the spirit of excellence is going to get the job. I also believe that the one who is chasing the false lottery God will stay broke and impoverished. The Bible promises, *"He who chases fantasies has poverty waiting for him"* (see Prov. 28:19).

## THE JOSEPH BLESSING

Not only must we know the truth about the connection between responsibility and blessing, we must also actively invite God into our business and careers. If a contractor will take the Holy Spirit on the job with him, he'll be far more proficient than he is in his own strength. I believe it wholeheartedly because I live this stuff.

Many times I find myself on my face, crying out for God to move in people's lives. I know there is nothing I can do on my own. So I'm crying out to Him, saying, "God, only You can satisfy them. Let them hear You because no words from my mouth can make a difference in their ears." I have seen Him move. I have seen Him give revelation. I have seen Him set feet to flight. It was not through my own strength that I saw lives changed. It was the Spirit of God working through me that brought transformation.

What's my point? You need to bring Him with you to help you accomplish whatever you do. He wants to bless the work of your hands, just like He blessed Joseph. He prospered Joseph in a prison. He prospered Joseph as a slave and as a foreman. He blessed Egypt because of Joseph (see Gen. 39-41). And now He is raising up Josephs in the marketplace. The question is, will you be faithful, as Joseph was, to call upon His name, which is above every other name? Will you call upon the gifting that He has stored up for you in Heaven? He wants to open up the storehouses and give it to you if you're willing to be diligent with what you already have.

Have you ever asked God to give you favor? Have you ever asked God to bless you? Have you ever asked God to grow your business beyond your ability? Have you ever asked God to give you supernatural ability?

That's what I have done. Since I rededicated my life to the Lord in 1993, God has given me supernatural ability. I know it's supernatural because there is no way in the natural that this former broke and homeless cocktail waitress, who was saved by grace, could do these things.

You were called for such a time as this. Ask God to open the floodgates, to send His angels, to bring strong people to your business.

Ask, "God please give me supernatural ability to hear and to absorb and to catch what I need to catch so that I can run with it. Give me supernatural faith, God. I promise to run with whatever You plant in me."

Revival is going on right now in the marketplace; many lost and suffering and hopeless people in the marketplace need a real touch from a real God. We have the right to ask. God wants us to invite Him into our workplaces and watch Him use us to change lives. We have far too often limited an infinite God who has some funny ways of doing things. We have tried to outline how and where He can operate. It's pathetic. Fortunately, God is breaking us out of our boxes so we can see who He is and what He wants to do through us.

## OUT OF THE BOX

God wants us to stop putting Him in a box. And He knows how to "bait the hook" in order to get us to do it. He has huge plans for our lives, things that defy our boxes. And He works in spite of us for our good.

For example, God brought my husband and me together through—lust! He took our unholy desires and used them to position us for His purposes. Now look at what we do. We wage war on the marketplace, sent by Almighty God.

Here's another example. God got me to come back to Him through—greed! He knows what to bait the hook with. He's smarter than you and me. He's infinitely intelligent. He put greed on the hook that caused me to turn back to Him while I was losing everything and I needed help. "Salvage my company please, before I lose it all," I prayed. It was absolute greed. God caught me in my sinfulness, saved me, and taught me to love Him.

Do you put God in a tiny box that says, "He'll only bless me if..."? Get Him out of the box.

*Thank you again for reminding me that I need to keep it simple. Thank you also for reminding me that it doesn't matter how long it takes me to get there, just to get there.*

—LESIA C

CHAPTER 3

# CALLED AS KINGS

In December of 1997, I had just given birth to baby number four and was enjoying all that comes with motherhood and taking care of a family. Hans and I attended a church of about 7,000 people that was an hour from where we lived, but we enjoyed the teaching, and that more than made up for the long commute.

One Sunday, our pastor got up and gave one of the most memorable sermons I've ever heard. He was grieved when he said, "I am here today to repent." He continued, "All of you that are in business, please stand up." Hans and I stood up with the business owners in the crowd. There were a lot of us.

Tears were streaming down his face and he said, "The Lord

gave me a revelation that you have the same anointing I have. You are a king in the marketplace, and we have prostituted this pulpit. We have sold this pulpit, saying that this is the ultimate success, but the Lord showed me that there are some called to be priests and there are some called to be kings.

As my pastor did this he asked us all to forgive him.

## MY REVELATION

Right after I dedicated my life to the Lord, I became very confused. I was a business trainer; I taught people how to become wealthy. But after getting saved, as I taught people how to build their businesses, I believed that what I was teaching was useless for the Kingdom of Heaven.

I began to think, *Now that I'm a Christian, I should go to seminary and become a pastor because it's obvious that my gift is with people and that is what I'm supposed to do. Then again, I'm in California, I'm a woman, it is 1993, and I can't even think of one woman preacher.* Quickly I thought, *No, I don't think that's going to work,* and yet, I really thought that was what I was supposed to do.

I would offer my business training for free to the church, and the church would say things like, "Hey, we need nursery workers, we need youth workers, we need, we need, we need, we need, and we need." So, I'd say, "OK, maybe I'll go serve in the nursery." And I would serve here and there, but nothing felt right to me. Something was missing as far as what I did for God. I told them stories about how we had thousands paying off their debts, people were managing their time better so they could spend more time with family or with God, people's businesses were growing and becoming extremely profitable, and yet the answer was to volunteer in the nursery. I had five babies already, and the nursery didn't need training.

As time went on I began to feel more and more useless in the

Body of Christ. I was helping people in my business right and left. Marriages were being healed, families were being restored, people were making money, paying off debt, and actually coming to hear me at a training seminar, but I felt useless inside.

Everything became very clear to me the day that I was chosen for business and I was being used by God—I was not useless in the Body of Christ because I wasn't involved with traditional ministry. In fact, I was in ministry with all the fruit to prove that God was using our business to lead people to Him. We saw salvations by the thousands, physical healings, captives set free, and financial breakthroughs for our clients. I realized that He was with us the whole time, and that there was a purpose for our business that was far greater than we knew. My pastor's confession of limiting the anointing to a pulpit or the ministry profession opened a new realm of the Lord for me and my life.

You have an anointing. You may be a pastor (shepherd) of your company. Or maybe you're an evangelist in the marketplace. Perhaps, like me, you have felt useless in the Body of Christ. But that's going to change. God has a calling for you that will shock you, and your life will never be the same. My life certainly hasn't been the same since I have had this very freeing and empowering revelation.

No more separation between your God and your business. No more separation between the Church and the marketplace. Today is the day that true understanding on these matters is coming together. The true Word of God is going out like a storm to take the Kingdom of Heaven with violence, just like the Bible says (see Matt. 11:12). I hope you're ready.

## A NEW MANDATE

Eight years ago I retired from my business. I was sick and tired of selling the world in a pretty package. I was sick and tired of just talking about business all the time and teaching people how to make money. I looked into the Heavens and I said, "God, if I cannot use my mouth freely for You, I will not use it at all. If I cannot tell the truth about money, if I cannot tell the truth about You and what You've done in my life, then I will shut this mouth and do nothing with it." And I did. I walked away from an outrageous amount of income, an outrageous amount of notoriety, and an outrageous amount of thank yous and letters and cards and fame. I said, "I'm done. I'm out of here."

After I quit, I became a full-time mother, and I realized that I was miserable. It wasn't related to my mothering duties; I loved being a mom. But I felt a void in my life because I was denying what I love to do. Somehow, I got this religious thing in my head that said, "You have five children. You're supposed to be a full-time mom baking bread, rolling out pasta, making homemade pies, making everybody fat, and driving your kids crazy." I got that religious thing in my head that said, "You're a wife and a woman and this is where you belong: in the home!"

I do believe there are some women who enjoy that lifestyle and that's all they want to do. Some women think that's beautiful and wonderful, and for them it is—but that's not the mandate that God gave me. I love my children with my whole heart. I love training them up, and I'm proud of every single one of them, but I drove them crazy when I was home 24/7. I loved being a mom, but something in me needed to go out and make an impact on people's lives.

Six years ago I got a mandate from Heaven. Prior to that, I believed that I would never speak again. Then God gave it back to me, but this time it was renewed, refreshed, and refined. This time I was ready "for such a time as this!" (See Esther 4:14.) Hans and I stepped out into the marketplace and I said, "I'm only going to speak if I can tell the truth about my God and what He has done in my life." Now we have hundreds of thousands of clients, and I work part-time. That's all God; He did it. He brought the people. He made it happen. He moved the heavens and the earth to make His will come to pass.

## A PECULIAR PEOPLE

God is looking for a peculiar people. He wants to raise them up out of the bounds of religion and straight into a walk with Him and Him alone. He wants to commission them with His mandate. You are designed by the Designer, who planted in you a desire to succeed. He created you with a unique mandate, and it is not to be a nursery worker. I have nothing against being a nursery worker; many people serve in the nursery. But it is not the climax of your call to succeed. God has a mandate for you; it is about revival.

One day my husband came home with a book called *God@Work* by Rich Marshall. Every one of you needs this book. He's written volume one and two; you need them both. When I read the first three pages, I wept like a baby because it was speaking to me. It was speaking to what was in me, to the issues that had confused me for a long time.

What amazed me was that Rich Marshall was in the same church service that I recounted at the beginning of this chapter. I was there in that seat, holding my three-month-old baby boy, and somewhere in that auditorium Rich Marshall sat as well. What are the odds?

That morning the preacher had been impregnated with a message of repentance about the pulpit being prostituted and sold to be something that it's not. He went out and began to anoint kings in the marketplace. He began to raise people up. *God@Work* is a book about the revival that's been going on in the marketplace for years. It's a book about men and women who thought, like me, that they were supposed to walk away from their businesses and become something that they're not. They failed at "ministry" so they had to go back into the marketplace to get a job. Then they found themselves getting and making millions of dollars and furthering the Kingdom of Heaven.

God shut every door for them to be ministers, opened every door for them to succeed in the marketplace, and encouraged their gifts of witnessing to the guy at the water cooler or praying for the person on the phone. Signs and miracles erupted in that company. Do you want the fear of making money as a Christian broken off of you? You need to read *God@Work*, volume one and volume two, which are available at GodisWorking.com.

After I read that book, I began to find purpose in what I did. I realized that we so often have no idea what unity means. We want to do good and be good, but our frailty and our baggage from many different influences make it hard for us to understand unity. The truth is that God's idea of unity and humanity's idea of unity are completely different things. We use 10 percent of our brains; how in the world can we understand an infinite God?

Fortunately, God's unity is not conformity. God's unity is absolutely diversity in harmony. This applies not only to our clothing styles, but also to how we do "ministry."

Many of us somehow were taught that ministry is a separate calling, that only preachers are anointed to preach the Gospel and pray for the sick. We've wrongly believed that only the "super spiritual" people have the power and the authority to see God move. The *super spiritual* are perceived as those with titles, ordination papers, degrees from a well-known seminary, robes, and positions, who know all the right people in the same group. But God used random people who don't fit into much of man's criteria. He uses people based on their hearts. He did use King Nebuchadnezzar, but He called him His servant.

## INFLUENCE

One of the main things that a big business gets for its owner is influence. Influence, simply put, means that people are listening. People are following. Let's refer again to George Barna's book *Revolution,* which is about where Americans today get their influence. Barna says, "There are seven dominant spheres of influence." By the way, this is not his opinion, these are the facts. These spheres were identified through polling, through the testimony of the people answering the phone and answering the question, "Where do you get your influence?"

According to Barna's documentation, the seven dominant spheres of influence are: movies, music, television, books, Internet, law, and family. The second tier of influencers comprises entities: schools, peers, newspapers, radio, and business.[1] The Church didn't even make it into the top 20. Essentially, that means that the Church has no influence.

You might blame somebody or this, that, and the other thing for the Church's lack of influence. But I believe it's by design. It's by design that the top influencers are music and movies and business and radio and schools and Internet because God is raising up a peculiar people who will infiltrate those very places and bring the Gospel straight to every crack and crevice.

He is raising a peculiar people. Read Joel 2. Read Acts 2. You'll see what I'm talking about:

> *I will pour out my Spirit on all people. Your sons and daughters will prophesy, your old men will dream dreams, your young men will see visions. Even on my servants, both men and women, I will pour out my Spirit in those days* (Joel 2:28-29).

According to the facts, not according to Dani's opinion, the

Church has become irrelevant. I promise you that it's by design. God has a plan. You have no reason to lose hope because you are part of the hope.

The old strategy of church programs and buildings—of building more buildings and bigger buildings, of creating more programs and better programs, of recruiting more volunteers and committed members—has failed to take over our cities for God. The cities have been overcome by other influences.

But guess who has and always has had influence?

## WHO HAS THE INFLUENCE?

The kings have the influence. This is the way it worked in the Bible. The priests served the kings, not the other way around. The priests, through their relationship with the king and their relationship with God, would hear from God and would bring direction and a message to the king.

But the king had the voice with the people. The king was the voice box to the people, not the priest. The same is true today.

The priest (the pastor, the full-time minister) is supposed to influence the king, to raise him up, give him godly advice and good direction. The priest influences the king so that the king will be a light on a hill, so that the king will turn to his place of influence and shout from the mountaintops the direction from Almighty God. The kings have the influence in the marketplace.

Who's at the head of the Internet? Who's the head of the publishing industry? Who's at the head of every influencer that Barna listed? The kings are at the head of it all. They are the leaders, and leaders dominate the marketplace. God is looking for a peculiar people who want to run with Him, who want to take cities by storm. He wants a peculiar people who He can anoint for business because business is one of the chief influencers in our cities and in the world today.

Unfortunately, in a lot of Christian circles the kings (the businessmen and women) are put down and even belittled. They are not encouraged and mentored in their kingly anointing. Rather, the religious spirit has often incited remarks like, "Be careful that you don't sin; be careful of material things," or, "You shouldn't be driving that Mercedes." We have missed the point. And we have ostracized our kings. We have never given them the chance to explain how they have been able to use their influence and their possessions for the Kingdom. We have not wanted to believe that a Mercedes could be a useful witnessing tool.

## ENDNOTE

1.   George Barna, *Revolution* (Carol Stream, IL: BarnaBooks, 2005).

*Dani's training taught us how to become professionals. Get to First Steps to Success; it will change your business, it will change your life!*

—Joe T

## CHAPTER 4

# THE THREE-FRONTED BATTLE

One of the things I have learned is that we have a three-fronted battle that we are called to fight in the marketplace. God wants to powerfully use us to bring His Kingdom in the marketplace. Our spiritual warfare deals with gaining influence, making money, and producing excellence.

## GAINING INFLUENCE

Gaining influence is spiritual warfare. You have a message with influence, and God wants you to use it just as I am using my influence to give you a message right now. Influence enables you to produce a message that people are actually hearing. If you're wise, smart, and can be trusted with your mouth, then God will say, "If you will let Me use you, then I will speak a message through you to My people."

God is raising up a new breed of people, a peculiar people who are called by His name to do some amazing things. He is raising up kings in the marketplace because they have influence. God wants you to make money because money brings influence.

The world desires success, fame, power, and excellence. Why do we watch sports or go to the orchestra or the opera? It's excellence in action. The world desires these things. So when you go into the world and excel, when you gain success, fame, and power, the world wants to listen to what you're saying. They will listen to you talk about God.

God is looking for a peculiar people who will trust Him and who are called by His name, a people who will ascend to those places of influence, power, fame, and excellence. He knows that you will do what I do; you will point to the King of kings and the Lord of lords, and you will say, "I got to this platform because I was saved by grace." You will testify about what He has done in your life, just as I am testifying to you right now about what He has done in mine. That is what influence can do.

He is looking for a particular people who will give Him the glory that He deserves. He's looking for a peculiar people who will ask for incredible things. Through the influence that God has given to me and He has used me to plant seeds in tens of thousands of souls who have been led into the Kingdom of Heaven. But we get many e-mails from people who have given their lives to the Lord or received healing just through our Web site.

He is looking for a peculiar people who will trust Him and who will use what He has given them to say, "He has saved me by grace, and He has blessed me with everything I have. If you will serve Him, He will bless you too."

He's looking for a people whom He can cloak in everything that the world desires because underneath the cloak, underneath the diamonds, underneath the suits, underneath the business success, underneath it all is Jesus, the King of the marketplace.

He's calling you by name. He has a revival burning in the marketplace. People whom you know are lost and suffering, and they need a real God and not religion. You can show Him to them. God wants to give you influence.

## MAKING MONEY

Making money is spiritual warfare. Your heathen competitor, who would take those profits and use it for his own glory, greed, and gluttony, is no longer getting those profits. Instead you are, and you're someone who God can trust with the profits.

The profits that you're gaining in the marketplace, which your competitor is no longer getting because God has entrusted them to you, are no longer being invested in greed, pornography, excess alcohol, and such stupid things. No, you're giving your 10 percent to the Kingdom of Heaven because that's what He requires. Obviously your heathen competitor does not give 10 percent to the Kingdom of Heaven. No, he gives it to organizations that take all of the glory for the help.

For example, the Red Cross distributes aid in the name of the Red Cross, not the name of Jesus. So the Red Cross gets the glory for helping. Recently, Hans and I were approached to give to an organization at Christmas time that gave tricycles to disadvantaged kids. The pitch was that each bike would say that the gift was from the organization. We said we would donate under one condition, each bike must say it came from Jesus and not us. The Christian man who approached us was on the organization's board, and when he checked to get approval for our request, he was shocked. Originally, the organization was Christian, but now the board was split about our request. Half said sure, the gift can be from Jesus, and the other half said no way. We said no way will we give thousands of dollars unless the bikes were given in the name of Jesus. In our minds, Jesus must get the glory or no deal!

In the last few years, we have given seven figures into the Kingdom of Heaven. I'm not telling you that so that you'll be impressed with me. Be impressed with our intelligent God. The God who says, "I will trust you with money as long as you give Me My portion." God says we can keep 90 percent if we give Him 10. If you're smart, you say, "Sure. No problem. That's a good deal."

Of course, not every believer takes God at His word and gives Him what He requires. Are you robbing God by not giving Him 10 percent? If you aren't giving 10 percent, you can't call yourself a king. I'll tell you that right now. If you're robbing God, what you have is going to be taken from you because you can't be trusted with it. If you're not tithing, you're in trouble. You're expecting to make money, but you're robbing God so you can forget it. Repent today and start giving.

Can you imagine a group of kings, of people in the marketplace who are making an obscene amount of money and are living only on 10 percent because they don't need 90 percent? Think of how much they could give into the Kingdom! Hans and I live on less than 10 percent of our income. It's too much. We can get everything we need and more on less than 10 percent. We are able to give far more because we don't need all of the money.

Can you imagine a group of business people who are making an obscene amount of money, far more than they could ever have use for? Can you imagine having a business that you can walk away from for two straight months? Can you imagine your income not even being touched for those two months and all the while your business continuing to grow because God is the CEO? Imagine what you could do with that freedom.

You could take supplies into places like Africa or Thailand. You could actually take miracles with you. You could deliver help instead of just saying that God loves them and that you'll pray for them. You could live out the Gospel—bringing food to starving people before you preach to them. You could demonstrate the Gospel.

I'm not discounting prayer or evangelism. But I believe God is raising up a peculiar people who will do things differently. He is raising up kings in the marketplace who will make far more than they could ever spend, kings who can be trusted with that bounty. And He will send them into the nations, into places of need. He will call them to take their families for two months into those places, and they will feed the hungry. They will pray for the sick, and they will be healed. They will bring miracles and supplies; they will bring wisdom and knowledge about how to take care of the land. They will teach others how to prosper right where they're planted (they know how to do it; that's what they do in the marketplace). They will come home from these extended trips to businesses that are just fine.

God is raising up a peculiar people who are called by His name, who will glorify Him in their success, who will glorify Him with what they do, who will give Him the glory that is due to Him. He is raising up a people who He can send out to places like Thailand to free those captives in the sex trade.

We've been sending over $20,000 a month to a place that builds orphanages for babies. Do you think that's making a difference? Yes. I'm sure your $10 a month is helping too. But if you get serious and realize that you've been called to make a whole lot of money, you will be able to send something that is building shelter after shelter after shelter, that is setting thousands of captives free instead of just one. It's OK to send one. But I think that we can do better than that.

The Bible says that money is the answer to everything (see Eccles. 10:19). I didn't write that. You can argue with God about that.

## PRODUCING EXCELLENCE

People, especially Christians, often say to me, "You are a Christian; you should do your seminars for free." I have a problem with that. My doctor's a Christian, but he doesn't perform open-heart surgery for free. This is the lottery message in action. They have an expectation of poverty, which is getting something for nothing. Too many of us seek something for nothing. But if you're seeking something for nothing, you're going to get nothing.

This standard that so many Christians hold manifests itself in a lack of excellence. This is why almost anything that has a Christian label seems to be crappy. My husband had a vision for our business, and this is what he said, "If we're going to do this, we're going to produce the best possible training in the marketplace. And by the way, we're Christians. If you have a problem with that, go somewhere else."

The bottom line is, you will not be able to deny the results that we get. We went out, with the blessing of God, to compete head-to-head in the marketplace. We have gone out with the best that we had to give, not with half-hearted work or crappy training that doesn't work and gets no results.

Too many Christians, because of their poverty mind-set, start a program with the question, "What can we do for really cheap? What can we cut corners on? What can we do for free?" Poverty. Poverty. Poverty. That's not how it should look in the Kingdom. A king competes head-to-head in the marketplace. A king takes new territory and new ground. A king goes into a city and transforms that city, not through crap, but through excellence.

When Solomon built the Temple, He brought the best. He brought the best workers. He brought the best craftsman. He brought the best artists. He brought the best ironworkers. He did not get crap (see 1 Kings 5-6).

How are we going to take the marketplace by storm? How are we going to do this? We're going to do it with guerilla warfare. Conventional warfare says this: "You see my ammo and my people, I see yours. OK, ready, 1-2-3." Guerilla warfare says this: "I look just like them, and I am sneaking into the enemy's camp. Before the enemy even knows, I've already set the captives free. Before he even realizes it, we are long gone."

We will win the battle through guerilla warfare in the marketplace. This means that we must infiltrate *everywhere.* Read Joel 2 again. He wants us everywhere, even in politics. Do you have a desire to be in politics? Where do you think that desire comes from? He wants us in politics. He wants us in music. He wants us on the television. He will use us in covert guerilla warfare.

People are tired of religion. They are tired of the traditional crap. They want excellence, they want success, and they want fame. He wants us in the marketplace because that's where the people are. And He wants us there with excellence.

Excellence attracts, results attract. And we have undoubtedly found that when you produce results for your clients in an excellent way you can say just about anything and they will still come back for more because they cannot deny the results they are getting from the training they are receiving. So in other words, they will "put up with" our Christian beliefs because what they have learned from us in the business realm or communication realm or financial realm has helped them get results.

We have heard them tell their friends and clients things like, "Go to Dani Johnson's First Steps to Success and it will explode your company and solve any problem you have, and oh, by the way, they are Christians, But don't let that stop you because the info she teaches you will show you how to pay off $25,000 worth of debt as I have just done in the last few months. Just ignore that she a Christian, because the training materials are phenomenal." So we have non-Christians promoting our content because we deliver the results that cause people's finances and relationships to grow exponentially, and the quality of their lives becomes something they didn't even know was possible.

## THE GREAT COMMISSION

What's the goal of this battle? The goal is not simply influence, money, and excellence. The goal is the Great Commission. You're supposed to use your profession for the Great Commission. The Bible is clear about what we are anointed for and what we are called to do. Isaiah 61:1 is my life purpose. It says:

> The Spirit of the Sovereign Lord is on me because the Lord has anointed me to preach good news to the poor. He has sent me to bind up the brokenhearted, to proclaim freedom for the captives, and release from darkness for the prisoners.

Have I not been preaching good news to the poor? That's what we're called to do. Our profession is to be used for the Great Commission.

Listen to these commissions from Jesus:

> Go into all the world and preach the good news to all creation (Mark 16:15).

> Peace be with you. As the Father has sent Me, I am sending you (John 20:21).

> All authority in Heaven and on Earth has been given to Me. Therefore go and make disciples of all nations, baptizing them in the name of the Father and of the Son and of the Holy Spirit (Matthew 28:18-19).

*I have given you authority to trample on snakes and scorpions and to overcome all the power of the enemy. Nothing will harm you* (Luke 10:19).

*Heal the sick, raise the dead, cleanse those who have leprosy. Drive out demons. Freely you have received, freely give* (Matthew 10:8).

*...Nothing will be impossible for you* (Matthew 17:20).

That is what we're supposed to do. We have been given the authority; we have been given the right; now we must go fight.

Of course, the verses listed flesh out in many different ways in our daily lives. As kings committed to the Great Commission, here are ten things that we're supposed to be doing:

1.  **Give** generously.

2.  **Influence** people properly and point them straight to Jesus.

3.  **Pray for the impossible**. Walk toward your miracle. Don't sit and wait; start walking. Look for opportunities to pray for your coworkers and employees. As a company, we start every work day with prayer.

4.  **Take risks.**

5.  **Trust God** and not your ability or your talent. I used to trust in my talent and my ability. I no

longer trust in either. My talent and my ability might be OK; however, my God's ability and talent and gifting are absolutely *endless*. Only He can satisfy.

6.    **Pray for others.** When you see a need, give your testimony about what God has done for you; pray for them, prophesy over them, and encourage them.

7.    **Worship Him and Him alone.** I've studied the kings in the Bible for about five years now. I will tell you the biggest mistake that they made, which caused the anointing and protection of the Lord to leave them. They worshiped other gods. Greed is idolatry. Your talent, if you idolize it and place your hope in it, is idolatry. If you have believed that you are supposed to be broke and be nothing and no one, that is idolatry, and it's time to repent. It's time to tear down the places of idolatry. Tear down the high places in your life. Perhaps you think, "I can't make it. I can't do it. I will fail. I'm not supposed to be here." That is idolatry; you are on the altar. Anything that exalts itself higher than the knowledge of God must be torn down. The thought, "I can't make it. I don't have what it takes. I wish there was a different way. I wish they would give it away for free," exalts your knowledge higher than the knowledge of God. God says, *"I have called you."* The knowledge of God says, *"Go forth into all the world and preach the good news to the poor."*

Today you will repent for idolatry. You will tear down the high places; that is your mandate as a king in the marketplace.

8.  **Be excellent.** You are to produce the best that you can and compete head-to-head with the top leaders in the marketplace. You have the spirit of the Living God in you; He will give you designs, He will give you strategies, He will give you inroads, if you ask Him.

9.  **Seek God for everything.** David inquired of the Lord left and right. Proverbs 3:5-6 says, *"Trust in the Lord with all your heart and lean not on your own understanding; in all your ways acknowledge Him and He will make your paths straight."* That must be what your life is about. As a king, one who has been blessed with much, much is required from you. God will bless you, but you better stay nestled right up next to Him or you're going to get yourself into some trouble.

10. **Act as a king.** Heal the sick; cast out demons; bring sight to blind eyes; let the deaf hear; set the captives free. That is your mandate from Heaven. That is your calling from Almighty God. He is raising up a peculiar people who are called by His name, who will succeed by His hand, who will be diligent, and who will be wealthy because of their diligence. He promises that a peculiar people that will go in every crack and crevice to reach somebody, they will be people who have

a mandate to take the Kingdom of Heaven violently by storm.

So imagine what could happen in your life if you are willing to
pray, to seek, to be diligent, to work with excellence, and to give.
Dream about what might happen if you committed yourself to taking
the marketplace by storm and bringing excellence in your sphere of
influence.

*You are truly blessed and anointed by God! Some of this info isn't a "new word," but it's a "now word" that's very relevant and needed. Your teachings have turned my life around. Continued blessings to you!*

—BECKY J

## CHAPTER 5

# THE TRUTH ABOUT MONEY

You will never enjoy total freedom without God. You must have God in your life to experience true freedom—that's the bottom line. Since you're reading this book, I know that you are anticipating learning something that will change your finances and even your life. You may even have within you a hunger and desire for change that you don't understand. Perhaps you have felt like you're under a cloud of confusion concerning money. Don't worry; you're not alone.

I think the most famous quote about money that I've ever heard is, "Money is the root of all evil." Well that's a lie from the pit of hell! Nowhere in the Bible will you find the saying that money is evil.

You won't find that. It does say that the *love* of money is the root of all kinds of evil (see 1 Tim. 6:10), but we've already covered that. It's idolatry, and God will not bless it.

In fact, my Bible says that money is the answer to everything. In Ecclesiastes 10:19 it says, *"...Money is the answer for everything."*

## WRONG VIEWS ON MONEY

According to Scripture, poverty and wealth are choices. Your God-given freedom is to be able to make choices in your life, and you can choose whether you want poverty or wealth. Unfortunately, many in the Church have chosen poverty because of their wrong views on money.

First, I want to clarify that the Bible does not say that God made you for poverty. It doesn't say that. What it does say is that He made Abraham and Isaac and many others rich. If God designed you for poverty, it makes no sense that most of the men and women in the Bible were extremely rich.

Years ago, after walking away from God and then coming back, I earnestly went before God and said, "You know what, God? What can I do for you? I'm a business woman. I present business training and life-sustaining seminars. I prepare people to do better in the marketplace. What in the world can I do for You?" I was struggling with the disconnect that I talked about in Chapter 3. I didn't understand that God wanted to be in my profession, to use my work for His Kingdom.

The Bible is very clear about what happens between God and the marketplace. It creates no disconnect between God and what you do for a living. In fact, in Colossians 3:23 we are told, "Whatever you do, work at it with all your heart, as working for the Lord, not for men." That's only one of the many business references found in the Bible.

Too many of God's people are held captive in a pew, doing

nothing with their gifts and their callings and what they've been prepared, from the day of their birth, to do. Many of them are not using their gifts because they don't fit into the corporate structure of the Church. Most of them are not called to full-time ministry as a traditional minister. But God has given each of us a gift (not just the pastors), and we're to utilize it and prosper, which is what I am going to show you how to do.

Many people in the Church are asking, "What can I do that's purposeful?" And many of them secretly, strongly desire to make a whole lot of money. They need to be freed to understand that God wants them to be wealthy and that He has a purpose for all of that money.

We are faced with conflicting views of money. Half of our culture says, "Get it, get it, get it, more, more, more now, now, now, now." The other half says, "Oh no. Be careful. Ouch. Did you see them? They're driving a Lexus. Oh God, have mercy on their souls." But neither is right. We must be careful not to prejudge others. We don't know what's in their hearts—maybe they live on 10 percent of their income and they give 90 percent.

You see, greed does not have an amount. You don't have to be rich to be greedy. And you don't have to be greedy to be rich. Have you ever looked at the wealthy and prejudged them for being wealthy? Maybe you've even thought, "All those wealthy people are power-hungry idiots. They're greedy people and don't deserve to have that much money." If you've ever thought or spoken those words, you may not realize it, but in judging others, you've judged yourself. In cursing others because they are rich, you curse yourself.

How can God give you wealth if you have cursed the wealthy? If you have said or thought that about the rich, you have an issue that you need to take care of. Not only do you need to seek forgiveness for thinking that way, but you need to stop saying those negative things and deal with your heart issue about passing judgment in the first place.

It's easy for people who are broke, especially Christians, to judge the wealthy and to use the Scriptures to justify their finances. Check your heart and make sure that isn't you.

## GOD'S FINANCIAL KINGDOM

Whether you know it or not, there is a financial kingdom. The people who succeed in the financial kingdom, for the most part, are following the rules. But I have found that you can even follow a few of the rules, while messing up on a few, and God's grace is so sufficient that He lets you try again, and again, and again, and again. In essence, life is just one big test.

There are two extremes in the financial kingdom: poverty and wealth. In Proverbs 22:2, it says, *"Rich and poor have this in common, the Lord is Maker of them all."* Rich and poor, the Lord has made us all. Not only that, but He's given us the choice of which one we'll be. Keep reading, and I'll show you how it's true.

Are you in the poor line? I know what that feels like because I grew up poor. My mom was on welfare. I was on welfare when I was 18. But the Bible says clearly that God is the respecter of no person. He shows favoritism to no one. That is powerful! That means that the wealthy do not have some kind of special favor. They're not God's favorites. We think, "If they're blessed like that, they must be God's favorites, right?" But that's not what the Bible says.

Since God is not a respecter of anybody and doesn't show favoritism to anyone, that means that it's an equal playing field. That means that our position in the financial kingdom (and everything else for that matter) is up to us. The financial kingdom boils down to you and the choices you make. *The fruit of our choices show up in our finances.*

Let's look at both sides of the financial kingdom so that you will be able to see clearly which side you're on and, if necessary, how to get to the other side.

## SEVEN STEPS TO POVERTY

First Samuel 2:7 says, *"The Lord sends poverty and wealth. . . ."* Did you think it was man? The Lord sends it. He humbles, and He exalts. He raises the poor from the depths and lifts the needy from the ash heap. He seats them with the princes and has them inherit a throne of honor. Do you want to be one of those whom He exalts? If so, you need to change some things in order to avoid poverty.

Let's discuss what the Bible says about poverty and some lifestyle choices and characteristics that lead one to poverty. In this section, I will point out many Scriptures in the Bible that explain poverty. These are only a sampling. I have studied every Scripture that talks about being poor and poverty, and I have found seven recurring themes. So here's a formula for poverty.

### Step 1:  Be Lazy and Halfhearted

Be lazy and work halfheartedly unto yourself or unto your boss and there is a guarantee that poverty awaits you.

Proverbs 6:9-11 says:

> *How long will you lie there you sluggard? When will you get up from your sleep? A little sleep, a little slumber, a little folding of the hands to rest and poverty will come on you like a bandit and scarcity like an armed man.*

I love that Scripture.

Proverbs 28:19 says, *"He who works his land will have abundant food, but the one who chases fantasies will have his fill of poverty."* (See also Prov. 14:23-24.) Twenty-five percent of people in this great nation cite the lottery as their plan for financial independence. Can you believe that? A poll asked people, "What is your plan for financial independence? What is your retirement plan?" Twenty-five percent of the people responded, "Winning the lottery."

### Step 2:   Be a Fool

In the Bible, foolishness is often associated with drunkards, gluttons, and wasteful people. Anyone who embraces these things and other foolish behaviors is embracing poverty. Proverbs 21:17 says, *"He who loves pleasure will become poor...."* Those who love pleasure will foolishly spend everything they have to get instant pleasure.

Proverbs 17:16 says, *"Of what use is money in the hand of a fool since he has no desire to get wisdom?"* Money without wisdom only leads you on a path that you don't want to travel.

Proverbs 17:20 says, *"A man of perverse heart does not prosper...."* What is perversion, and what does it have to do with foolishness and the financial kingdom? "A perverse heart" could imply the perversion of truth, as in, *"The love of money is a root of all kinds of evil"* (1 Tim. 6:10) being perverted into, "money is evil." But a "perverse heart" can also be found in other areas of your life where you've taken something pure and twisted it for pleasure or immoral purposes (pornography, adultery, illegal business dealings, and so forth).

The Bible talks about meekness. Specifically, it says that the meek will inherit the earth (see Ps. 37:11; Matt. 5:5). Man has interpreted that Scripture to mean that you must be poor to be meek. That also is perversion. Such perversions of God's truth are a foolish reliance on human understanding instead of God's understanding. And they will only bring poverty.

### Step 3:   Be Prideful in Prosperity

If you have pride during times of prosperity, forgetting God, it will lead you to poverty. Deuteronomy 28:47-48 says:

> *Because you did not serve the Lord your God joyfully and gladly in the time of prosperity, therefore in hunger and in thirst, in nakedness and dire poverty, you will serve the enemies the Lord sends against you....*

This is powerful. Think about God's warning. During a time of prosperity, God wants the glory. He wants you to bless Him. Throughout history and throughout the Scriptures, before a time of repentance, God would lavish His children with great prosperity to turn their hearts toward Him (see Prov. 21:14-15). He desired to bring repentance through blessing.

His first method of correction was to bless abundantly so that people would fall to their knees and say, "God we don't deserve this. Thank you Lord for what you've done. Your goodness is overflowing. Your grace is more than sufficient. Your mercy just completely blows my mind." Unfortunately, He never heard these words.

Instead, people became full of themselves and greedy for more, more, more. Have you ever been hungry, thirsty, naked, in dire poverty, and serving your enemies? I have, and it stinks. We must be careful to remember and honor God in our prosperity.

### Step 4:   Hide Your Sins

Proverbs 28:22 says, *"A stingy man is eager to get rich and is unaware that poverty awaits him."* Proverbs 13:21 says, *"Misfortune pursues the sinner, but prosperity is the reward of the righteous."* Basically, these Scriptures say that if you attempt to hide your wrongdoing you will realize poverty. Proverbs 13:18 says, *"He who ignores discipline comes to poverty and shame....”* So poverty is also connected to our disobedience; it is a fruit of rebellion.

### Step 5: Love Money

The love of money, otherwise known as greed, will bring on poverty. If you desire money more than you desire anything else, more than God, more than your kids, more than your spouse, then guess what? Poverty will show up at your doorstep.

Ecclesiastes 5:10 says, *“Whoever loves money never has money enough....”* That's how you know if you have greed in your heart. No matter how much you make, it's never enough. You are never satisfied with what you have. That is called having a spirit of greed. I was once absolutely plagued and possessed by a spirit of greed. But now I can say that there is no price that someone could pay me to do something that my Daddy in Heaven has not led me to do. Nothing. I will not compromise my walk with Him for a price tag. Ten years ago, it was a totally different story.

*“Whoever loves money, never has money enough.”* The rest of Ecclesiastes 5:10 says, *“... Whoever loves wealth is never satisfied with his income. This too is totally meaningless.”* Are you completely satisfied? Or do your attainments never seem to be good enough? No matter what you do, every time you hit a goal, it never seems to be good enough. Do you feel that you are constantly falling short? Be honest with yourself. If you're never satisfied with your things, possessions, or money, then you're plagued with greed.

Greed is a wicked, wicked, wicked deceiving, crafty, evil spirit that will make you do things that you never even thought were possible (if you've submitted yourself to that spirit of greed). So if you feel like you don't have enough, it's only going to hurt you.

Matthew 6:24 says, *“No one can serve two masters. Either he will hate one and love the other, or he will be devoted to the one and despise the other. You cannot serve both God and money.”* That's the truth. You cannot serve both God and money. But you can serve the God who has the money. It's all about where your heart and affections are.

First Timothy 6:10 says, *"For the love of money is a root of all kinds of evil."* It's the *love* of money, not money itself. You know you love money and wealth if you're never satisfied with it. If it is a deep hole within you that never seems to be filled, that means you are worshiping a spirit of idolatry instead of God Almighty.

Colossians 3:5 says that greed is idolatry. The reality is that we live in a nation that has more idolatry than any other nation on the face of the planet. Our idolatry is far more subtle than the idolatry in India.

In the United States, idolatry is rampant. We admire songwriters and singers. We idolize sports figures, movie celebrities, preachers, speakers, anyone in high-level positions. Your kids have little idols (action figures) in their toy chests. I'm being serious. We have idolatry all over the place. We teach our kids idolatry, and we don't even realize it. This idolatry is a manifestation of our greed. We need to watch out for this stuff.

The Bible also says that a greedy man brings trouble to his family, but that he who hates bribes will live (see Prov. 15:27). Proverbs 28:25 says, *"A greedy man stirs up dissension, but he who trusts in the Lord will prosper."*

Luke 12:15 says, *"Watch out. Be on your guard against all forms of greed. A man's life does not consist in the abundance of his possessions."* Where does greed lead? It leads to poverty. It leads to wickedness. It leads to destruction. It leads to all those things.

So you may wonder, can we enjoy wealth without being greedy? Yes. Listen to me carefully. Greed and wealth are not the same thing. You can have wealth without being greedy. You can also have greed without being wealthy (and many people do). And as we've read, the Bible teaches that those who are both wealthy and greedy will not remain wealthy. Labeling all wealth as greed is a perversion. And according to the Bible, a perverse thought will be impoverished (see Prov. 17:20).

### Step 6:  Be Selfish and Stingy

This is an absolute formula for poverty. People who do not give will be impoverished. And don't worry, I am not a pastor of a conventional church who is saying this to prep you or sell you on sending in an offering. I am a wealthy businesswoman who works for a living, and God blesses the work of my hands.

Proverbs 28:22 says, *"A stingy man is eager to get rich and is unaware that poverty awaits him."* Sometimes we're stingy and we don't realize it. You can know if you're stingy by looking at your fruit. Your fruit will show you what kind of seed you planted. If poverty is your fruit, then stinginess and hording are seeds that you have planted. Stinginess is a poverty mentality. Stinginess is a choice; if you choose to be stingy, you choose to be poor— by choice.

Proverbs 28:27 says, *"He who gives to the poor will lack nothing, but he who closes his eyes to them receives many curses."* Do you really believe that? "He who gives to the poor will lack nothing." Stingy people do not give to the man on the street. Stingy people do not pour money into charitable organizations. If you are not currently giving to someone, you, my friend, are stingy. And what follows stinginess? Poverty.

### Step 7:  Be Fearful

Fear will lead you to poverty. There are several stories in the Bible that show us that fear leaves us impoverished, and even the extreme poverty of death. In the Book of Numbers, chapter 13, we see 12 spies sent to look at a prosperous land that was promised to their forefathers by God, a land flowing with milk and honey. A land with everything their hearts could have ever desired, and then some. Ten of the spies were afraid, and two were not. The ten were not permitted to enter the land because of their fear that led to another sin that eventually led to their deaths and the death of many others who followed them. The two—Joshua and Caleb—who did not fear but took risk in acting on their faith, they received the Promised Land and all the prosperity of it.

## GOD'S TEN STEPS FOR WEALTH

Is it possible for a Christian to be wealthy? Yes. The Word says that God created the poor and the wealthy (see Prov. 22:2). The Bible actually has many positive things to say about wealth and money.

Ecclesiastes 7:12 says, *"Wisdom is a shelter as money is a shelter...."* Ecclesiastes 10:19 says, *"A feast is made for laughter, and wine makes life merry, but money is the answer for everything."* This Scripture sets the record straight. *"Money is the answer for everything."* This offends many of you. How can money be the answer to everything? Let's examine this further.

Deuteronomy 28:63 says, *"It pleased the Lord to make you prosper...."* God is pleased to make us prosper. Perhaps this is hard for you to believe. If you have children, think about how you feel when you bless them, especially when they've done something good. Loving parents delight in blessing their children. Your Daddy in Heaven, who is perfect and unfailing in His love, desires for you to prosper.

This means, if you're not prospering, that you need to ask yourself, "Why not?" Here are some characteristics that God associates with prosperity.

Deuteronomy 29:9 says, *"Carefully follow the terms of this covenant [My commandments] so that you may prosper in everything you do."* God requires that we follow His commandments. Don't murder. Don't steal your neighbor's wife. Don't be greedy for other people's things.

Don't lie. Don't cheat. Don't steal (see Exod. 20:1-17). Jesus summed up the laws saying to love God and your neighbor.

Proverbs 11:25 says, *"A generous man will prosper...."* Proverbs 28:25 says, *"...He who trusts in the Lord will prosper."* Jeremiah 29:11 says, *"'For I know the plans I have for you,' declares the Lord, 'plans to prosper you and not to harm you, plans to give you hope and a future.'"*

Ezekiel 36:11 says, *"I...will make you prosper more than before...."* Genesis 39:2 says, *"The Lord was with Joseph and he prospered...."* Deuteronomy 30:5 says, *"...He will make you more prosperous...."* Job 22:21 says, *"Submit to God and be at peace with Him; in this way prosperity will come to you."*

These are just a sampling. More Scriptures speak positively of wealth and money than negatively. Based on my Bible reading, I believe there are ten steps associated with God's formula for wealth.

### Step 1:  Don't Love Money

If you are all consumed with money, if you worry about money, then money is an idol to you. If you worry about money, about how you're going to pay your bills, or about how you're going to take care of the mortgage, then in your life money has run ahead of God.

The Word of God tells us to take every thought captive and make it obedient to Christ (see 2 Cor. 10:5). In Matthew 6:25-34, it says (paraphrased), *"Do not worry about what you will eat or what you will wear because your God in Heaven already knows what you need."* There is no need to worry when you have faith. So if you're worried about money, it's nothing but a total deception from the pit of hell.

The enemy wants you to worry about finances, wants you to think about money in order to drive you away from God. He knows that if you actually follow God, if you actually honor Him, if you actually love Him, if you actually serve Him, then He will prosper you and make you great in the city gates. You'll be blessed going in, and you'll be blessed coming out (see Deut. 28:6). He will bless those who bless you, and He will curse those who curse you (see Gen. 12:3). The enemy of your soul knows this. He reads the Bible more than many of us do.

### Step 2:  Work With Excellence

In Colossians 3:23 it says, *"Whatever you do, work at it with all your heart, as working for the Lord, not for men."* (See also Proverbs 21:5.)

Most of us need some work in this area. But if you work with all your might as unto God, He is your boss. And when it comes time for promotion, it does not matter what a jerk of a boss you have ahead of you because God is over him or her. And God sees what you do. He sees your diligence. He sees the extra hours. He sees the motivation. He sees the heart that you're pouring into it. He sees, and He will bless the fruit of your hands. Don't worry about your boss. God will just promote you right above him.

Look at Joseph in the Bible. His story is so powerful. Joseph was blessed by his Father with a vision, and then he was thrown into a pit. He was then enslaved and brought to Egypt to be a slave in the house of a governor who worshiped a foreign god. And the Word says that God prospered him. He was then accused because of the governor's adulterous wife. "Ooh Joseph, come here honey." She looked at that fine young man and said, "I have to get me some of that."

And Joseph ran. He eventually was falsely accused of committing adultery and was put in prison. Then God exalted him from prison to become the head of the most powerful nation of that time (see Gen. 37-41).

So, you have nothing to worry about. It doesn't matter what man or woman is above you. It means nothing because God will bless the fruit of your hands *if* you are working as unto Him.

### Step 3:  Know Your Money's Purpose

You need to know that the money that God has blessed you with is for a much bigger purpose than your personal possessions. Certainly God wants to bless you with stuff. But He doesn't want the stuff to own your life.

Let me share my personal experience with greed. I was a woman whose stuff owned my life. During our twenties, Hans and I were living in this huge, 6,000-square-foot house and making a fortune. Life was good and everything felt wonderful.

One day I was preparing for a Bible study, and the Spirit of God came over me. I heard God say, "Who's this all for?" I started thinking. *I know it's not for my husband because he could live in a shack and be happy.* "Then who's it for?" I know it's God speaking to me, so I can't dance around the truth. *Well God, it's not for my kids because they don't need 10 acres. They don't need a tennis court. They don't need a guest house. They don't need a 6,000-square-foot house.*

"Well then who's it for?" Hmmm…I was running out of options. My cheeks were twitching. "Then who's it for?" *Well Lord, I guess You don't need it. You own everything.*

I had tricked myself into believing that it was to honor God. I was convicted. *I'm sorry, Lord. It's all about me. All my stuff, my cars, my jewelry, my clothes, my house was all about me and my ego trip.* In truth, it was the lifestyle that this homeless cocktail waitress had accumulated, and it was nothing more than a reflection of my big, fat, greedy ego trip. That's all it was. And you know what? I was empty inside.

No matter how much we made, it was never enough because we spent it faster than we made it. Here I loved God. I served God. I honored God. We paid our tithes. But it was all about, "Well, this is what I'm accustomed to. This is the kind of lifestyle we're used to."

In a single moment, that all changed when the Lord said to me, "Sell your things and follow me." Funny thing is, I had thought I was following Him. And instantaneously, I said, "I rebuke you devil in the name of Jesus, go back to hell where you belong!" He said, "This is Jesus and if you love Me, you will follow Me, and you will sell your things." I started weeping and fell on the floor and began to cry and repent because I realized that my whole life had become centered on me.

I went downstairs to tell Hans what God had just said to me. He was sitting at his computer, and He took one look at me and could tell something dramatic happened. He could tell this was going to be a long conversation, and he had this, "Don't bother me right now, I'm busy" look on his face. I went to him with tears streaming down my face and said, "Hans, I have to talk to you." He said, "What?" I said, "This is serious. God just told me that we need to sell the house."

We had just moved into the house three months before. We bought the house in a down market in an area that is not prosperous for real estate. We saved $300,000 by moving up to the mountains, and we got so much more than what we needed. When I said, "Hans, God told me we need to sell the house," his jaw dropped and he said, "God told me the same thing two weeks ago, but I told God He'd better tell you because I ain't fighting that fight."

So there we were in absolute agreement, broken before God. And God is so faithful. He exposed the greed that had crippled my life, and I hadn't even realized that I was walking through life crippled. I used to say I could walk away from it all tomorrow and that it meant nothing to me, until the day God told me to walk away from it.

But like I said, God is so faithful. I told you that we had bought the house in a down market in an area that is not prosperous for real estate. It had been in a ten-year slump at the time. And do you know what the Lord did? He brought us one buyer who needed to sell her house in order to buy our house. She had raised four children in a house that was built by a man who had raised four children. The land was totally set aside for God. These were godly people; a godly man had built the house, and a godly woman lived in the house. And she needed to sell her house in order to buy my house. In six months, there was only one person who came to buy our house, and it was this godly woman.

She was going to turn our dream house into a board and care home for developmentally disabled people. God Almighty is so loving and so faithful. He told us to sell the house, and then He prospered us in our obedience.

And He will prosper you if you're willing to work for it. He brought us one buyer who had a house that I hated, but I knew walking into it that it was underpriced about $50,000 on the market. I knew that just painting it and putting my stuff in it would raise the value instantaneously. Of course, I had to sell half of my stuff. I have scars on my toes from stubbing them in the little closet in my new bedroom. The new bedroom was smaller than my old closet. That was humbling.

God is full of love and grace and mercy; I was full of sin and greed and disgust and wickedness. And we made $100,000 on that house. God sold that house. We bought it. We lived in it for 11 months, and that was it. And we made $100,000 in a down market. That house currently has $150,000 of equity in it and is being rented by godly people whom God is working on as well.

I remember talking to my sister-in-law who used to complain about the house she lived in. I said, "I know exactly how you feel, but this house in this neighborhood has been the best thing that has ever happened to me because it was in this house where I was set free from greed."

It was in that house that I discovered every wicked, nasty, spoiled-rotten-brat thing that was in me. It was in that house that God set me free from something I had no idea I was in bondage to. And even now, since I've come out of retirement and we started speaking again, we have had companies offer us seven figures if I would only train for them because they did not want my mouth to train their competition.

"Dani, we'll pay you a million dollars a year. It'll be great. You will not have to build your own business. We'll just give it to you monthly if all you do is go on the road once a month for us." And because I am no longer driven by greed, I could look them in the face and say "Thanks, but no thanks." You might be thinking, "You are stupid." But I know that God has called me to do something else, and greed is not going to get in the way. That path has brought many millions more than what was offered, because we were not chasing it or consumed and owned by it.

When I was in the grips of greed, no matter how much we made, it was never enough because we spent faster than we made it. Here I was. I loved God. I served God. I honored God. We paid our tithes. But it was all about us. This is the kind of lifestyle we had grown accustomed to. Praise God, He delivered us. Now I know that my money has a purpose much bigger than me.

### Step 4:  Know It's God's Money

It's not yours. It's God's money. It comes from Him, and He has a much bigger purpose for that money. He wants to multiply that money, but when you get it and you don't honor Him or you're stingy with it or you're all caught up in it, He will not bless you with more. He won't give you more because those attitudes put you on a road to destruction. If you're on a road to destruction, He's not going to give you more so that you wind up destroying your life.

### Step 5:  Be Generous

Don't hoard. Don't be stingy. God wants to bless you with more, but He won't unless you're a giver. He loves a cheerful giver (see 2 Cor. 9:7).

We teach our kids to tithe because we don't want to deal with adult children who won't do what the financial kingdom calls them to do. (See Proverbs 11:24.) So our kids tithe their own money, their own earnings. Our daughter Arika often works with me. She will take 10 percent of what she earns and give it to God. Do you want God to trust you with more? Then give willingly. Give graciously. Give with a cheerful heart.

### Step 6:   Give Into the Right Soil

This is absolutely enormous. When I first learned this, my head just about exploded. In the Bible, it talks about the Parable of the Sower, which talks about four different types of soil into which a farmer will sow seed (see Matt. 13:1-23).

The first type of soil discussed is hard ground. When the seed is thrown on hard ground, the birds of the air come in and steal the seed away. The second type is rocky soil. If you sow seed on rocky soil, it will sprout quickly because the soil is shallow. But because it does not have a root system, it is scorched by the sun. It sprouts quickly, and it dies quickly.

The third soil is the thorny soil. In this type of soil, the plant puts down roots, but as it pops up, it is choked out by thorns. The fourth type of soil is fertile ground, and it is the only soil in which you want to plant your seed because it is the only place it will grow. The Bible says that fertile ground yields a return of 30-, 60-, and 100-fold (see Matt. 13:8).

Some of us are planting money in infertile soil. The Bible says that whatever you plant you shall reap (see Gal. 6:7). Perhaps you have noticed that your income hasn't increased. Maybe it has stayed the same. You have to think about where you are sowing your seed. You might ask, "How do you know where the ground is fertile?" You have to look at the fruit. If you want your money to return back to you a hundred fold, you have to sow it into fertile ground.

### Step 7:    Understand the Seasons

You need to realize that there is a time of plenty and a preparation for a time of famine. There are seasons of famine and seasons of plenty. That is absolutely scriptural. Joseph did this when God blessed his nation for seven years with great abundance (see Gen. 41:28-46).

Are you in a season of plenty? If you are, know that during the season of plenty you must not eat all of your seed. That season of plenty is for preparation so that you may still prosper when other people are failing all around you financially. In the Book of Genesis we see very clearly that that is how God has designed it.

If you're in a season of famine and you are prospering where you're planted and you can be trusted with what you have, you will gain more. That's how the financial kingdom works. If you're in that season of famine, you better take care of everything you have. Have a spirit of excellence during this time and God will cause you to prosper when other people are failing financially.

Remember what we learned earlier? The Bible says that if you forget Him in time of prosperity, poverty awaits you around the corner. So if you are in a prosperous situation right now, don't you dare forget who owns it and how He has blessed you.

### Step 8:    Prosper Where You're Planted

Do you have dreams and visions of where you want to go and what you want to do? Are there places that you'd like to visit? Have you become frustrated because your dreams haven't come to pass?

The enemy wants to get your focus on what you don't have instead of on how to make yourself prosper right where you are. This is how people do it. They have a dream. They say, "Dani, when I have this big business, then I'm going to lavish my people, and I'm going to take really good care of my customers. But these lazy, broke people, I can't stand them. They're driving me crazy."

Or I might hear, "Oh Dani, if my husband would act right, I

would do a lot better." "If my husband would act right, then I'd treat him better." "If my wife would stop nagging, then I'd buy her flowers once in awhile." It doesn't work that way. You have to prosper where you're planted under the current circumstance that you're in.

Joseph in the Bible had a gift to interpret dreams. He used that gift in a prison, and that's what got him promoted all the way to the top—he prospered where he was planted (see Gen. 41). Serving in the prison was not what he was designed to do. But during the time in the prison, he was equipped to run a nation, the most powerful nation at that time.

### Step 9:  Ask Big

God is not a small God. His arms are not short, and His ears are not deaf (see Isa 59:1). The Bible clearly says that no mind has conceived, no eye has seen, and no ear has heard what God has in store for those who love Him (see 1 Cor. 2:9).

You need to think bigger than what you're thinking. You need to think wider and taller than what you're thinking. And you need to ask according to God's size, not your size. I'm asking God for millions of lives from all over the world. That's what I'm asking for.

"God, please let me have the platforms where I can affect millions of people's lives from all over the world. I'm asking that it won't stop there, but that they will go and they will affect millions upon millions of people's lives. That millions and millions of homes will be made right and come into right standing with You and principles that work."

Part of asking big is asking for help. The Bible says that if you need wisdom, you should ask for it (see James 1:5). If you don't know how to do something, ask and He will give you the understanding you need.

### *Step 10: Learn From the Wise*

It's OK to make mistakes. There are ups and there are downs. In the down time, don't worry. Don't fret. Don't freak out. Just know that you are fully taken care of, that God loves you. God will cause you to prosper. You will have rainy days. You will make some mistakes, so I want you to write this down: *It's OK if you mess up.* It's OK. God's Word says that His grace far exceeds the Heavens (see Ps. 103:10-12 and Prov. 12:15; 13:20; 15:12). That is huge. His grace is enormous.

Often the only understanding of grace that we have is the grace that our friends or our family shows us, and that's usually pretty pathetic. A small amount of God's grace reaches to the Heavens. The Word says that grace is never ending, which means that we have the grace to fail and to fall right into His arms. He will brush off your knees, put you back on your feet again, and say "It's OK. Go at it again." How awesome is that?

Don't do what most people do in a time of failure, and give in or give up. Failure shows you something. It shows you where you have some things to shore up—some skills you are missing, some things you needed to learn, some knowledge that you need to invest into. My husband and I have made countless mistake—more than you or anyone could know. From those mistakes we have postured to learn and grow. We both have humbled ourselves countless times and have invested into countless seminars to learn from other wealthy people. We have also asked those with positive results in areas that we wanted to master such as marriage, parenting, finances, and business how they have done it.

What I have found is that most people's egos are so big that they will not humble themselves or posture themselves to learn from others who have succeeded at something that they want to accomplish. Instead, when they fail many people blame the economy, spouse, or even their kids. Some blame the business and say things like, "I've tried those things before and they didn't work for me." The truth is they didn't really work at whatever they wanted.

As I mentioned previously, in all of my sin, in all of my greed, God still blessed me financially. He did it because He is looking for an obedient heart that will fall into His arms instead of depending on its own strength. His grace is more than enough. That, to me, is absolutely awesome.

## INVITATION

The financial kingdom spreads far and wide, but the head of that Kingdom is God. He is inviting you to follow His steps toward prosperity. Will you submit to Him so that He may bless you, so that He may prosper you as He wants to prosper you? He desires you to be in good health (see 3 John 1:2).

God wants to see His people freed from all bondage, including financial bondage. God does not want you to be in financial bondage. Are you tired of financial bondage? Do you want to be free from it? You need to commit your ways to Him and live according to the standards of the financial kingdom.

*You have amazing tips that are simple and doable.*
*As an art teacher of 800 young children from first*
*through eighth grade, whom I teach week after*
*week, I thought I knew how to teach until I saw you*
*teach! Now I am using your teaching techniques in*
*the classroom, and they work!*

—STELLA D

CHAPTER 6

# RECEIVING HIS ANOINTING

In this chapter we're going to take a break from talking about money and talk about a subject that has affected many Christians in the marketplace. I briefly touched on it in Chapter 3, but here I want to examine it further. It is something that I've studied and studied. The more I have studied it, the more I am convinced of this monster revelation. It has completely changed my life. I would not be here today had I not learned this particular truth.

## OUT OF PLACE

I spent many years as a Christian businesswoman feeling

completely insignificant in the Kingdom of Heaven. I felt like, "I'm a speaker, so I must get into some kind of ministry. That must be what I'm supposed to do." However, every time I attempted to try to do something for God, nothing ever opened up. As I shared in the last chapter, the Church never gave me a platform to speak on, not even at a woman's retreat. I felt so out of place.

My husband also felt out of place. We didn't feel called to the nursery. We didn't feel called to the children's ministry. We didn't even feel called to the youth ministry. There was no place for people like us. God prospered us greatly in the business world, filled up convention centers with people for us to speak to, and yet, I would have gladly done a Bible study for nine people.

What I bought into was the lie that I was never going to be good enough for God: I wasn't pure enough for God; I wasn't holy enough for God; I wasn't righteous enough for God; God could never use me. I believed that I just was not called to spread the Word in which I so passionately believed.

Through my business, I had the chance to lead a whole lot of people to Him and to help a lot of people get back on track with Him. God gave me the chance to talk about the thing that I am most passionate about: Him. I was able to help people get on track with God, make their lives right, and follow godly principles that really do work.

The principles that I share about success are in the Bible. I was serving God by teaching them. But I didn't recognize it as ministry. I always felt there was no place for me. Have you ever felt that way? Have you ever said, "There's no place for me in _____"? I said to God eight years ago, "God, if I cannot use my mouth for your glory, I will not use it at all," and I went back to folding my arms.

If I cannot tell the truth about success, if I cannot tell the truth about money, if I cannot tell the truth about God, then I don't want to use this tongue to speak about anything. It's not worth it for me. It's empty. I lived in the big fancy houses, had big jewelry, big clothes, big everything. I was just a spoiled rotten brat, and it was empty.

So the long and the short of it is this: it was my dream to be able to stand and tell the truth. I wanted to be able to speak on our own platform, without being controlled by any company or church leader, without having anyone control the message. My message is what it is, and if they don't like it, they don't have to come back. I don't care because they're not my provider. My God is, and that's the way I saw it.

So what I truly believe, beyond a shadow of a doubt, is that the Church has done a great job but that in the last days it has become irrelevant in some places. The pulpit has been the thing that has been promoted. Only those who are really "super spiritual" are allowed to speak from the pulpit. Only those who are very "holy" get the title of reverend or pastor. That was what I thought I was working toward. I thought, *If I get good enough, then someday I'll be able to be that.* I was striving for something that I wasn't called to, not realizing that God had a different plan for me.

But since then, I have discovered that there is a revival going on in the marketplace. Did you know that? You're in one, and you don't even realize it. God is looking for a chosen people, a chosen generation after His own heart, who will be used in a mighty way out in the marketplace. Many business people wouldn't be caught dead in a church. I was one of them. Too many have been badly wounded by the Church. They've been held back, not fed, just used.

Have you ever been wounded by the Church? I'm not bashing the Church. I love my brothers and sisters, but the reality is that they are people just like the rest of us, and people make mistakes. Unfortunately most people look at people in church and think, "Well, you're supposed to be perfect." That's our fault for even thinking that. That's stupid. We shouldn't have those kinds of high expectations for them. But they should also live with a higher respect level. They make mistakes; we all do.

Anyplace you put people, you're going to find mistakes. That's the reality. So it's not up to us to look at the Church and say, "You should be more perfect. You should be more holy. You should be more of this." No. We should step up and say, "I'm going to give it my best shot wherever I'm at."

The unfortunate thing, something that my husband and I are very passionate about, is that there's very little equipping for people like you and me who are out there in the war zone every single day. How do I, as one who loves God, serve Him in my work?

When I rededicated my life to the Lord, I thought, "What's my use?" As I stated in Chapter 3, I felt totally insignificant, like there was nothing I could do for God. And as my heart grew more and more in love with Him, my desire to move in His will increased and the gifts of the Spirit grew. The more insignificant I felt, the more I felt like, "I'll never make it to this position. I was never called to preach every week to the youth. I never felt called to the nursery." I just never felt called to any of that stuff, and my husband and I felt insignificant and almost guilty because we felt like we were not serving God with what we were doing. I felt like I would never make it through the church's "corporate structure."

## BEYOND THE PULPIT

The question I eventually came to was, why do we make this little box called *religion?* The word *religion*, when it is translated from the Greek, means "bondage." Religion was created by man.

Yet we've taken the Bible, applied it with our own selfish motives, and put people in a box called *religion.* We've put them in this little place and said, "You better look like this, dress like this, and you shouldn't say stuff like that or you're going to get in trouble."

Have you ever felt useless? Have you felt like your gifts and talents have no purpose? If so, it's because we men and women have created this false structure, a structure that does not exist in the Bible. We've created walls to act out our spirituality, and those walls need to come down.

Those walls need to be dozed, as they say where we come from. It is time to pull the dozers out because there are too many captives who think they have no talent. There are too many captives who think they are useless.

In First Corinthians 12, we learn about spiritual gifts and our role in the Body of Christ. This passage is not an exhaustive list of the gifts of the Spirit (we will examine the 15 gifts and their position later). There are things listed that you have and that you don't know you have. As we go through this information, you will discover that you have many of these gifts and you don't even know it. You will also discover who gave them to you and what they are for. Get ready because you may be shocked!

First Corinthians 12:4 reads:

> *There are different kinds of gifts but the same Spirit. There are different kinds of service but the same Lord. There are different kinds of working but the same God works all of them in all men.*

Take note of the word *all*. That includes you.

First Corinthians 12:7-11 says:

> *Now to each one, the manifestation of the Spirit is given for the common good. To one there is given through the Spirit the message of wisdom, to another the message of knowledge by means of the same Spirit, to another faith by the same Spirit, to another gifts*

*of healing by that one Spirit, to another miraculous powers, to another prophecy, to another distinguishing between spirits, to another speaking in different kinds of tongues, and to still another the interpretation of tongues. All these are the work of one and the same Spirit, and He gives them to each one, just as He determines.*

Verses 14-19 of that same chapter go on to say:

*The body is not made up of one part but of many. If the foot should say, because I'm not the hand, I do not belong to the body, it would not, for that reason, cease to be part of the body. And if the ear should say, because I'm not the eye, I do not belong to the body, it would not, for that reason, cease to be part of the body. If the whole body were an eye, where would the sense of hearing be? If the whole body were an ear, where would the sense of smell be? And in fact, God has arranged the parts in the body, every one of them, just as He wanted them to be.*

First of all, the Bible says that God gives gifts to all people (see 1 Cor. 12:4). That includes you. Exodus 31:3 says, *"I have filled him with the Spirit of God, with skill, ability and knowledge in all kinds of crafts."* God has given you abilities.

Remember what it says in Matthew 25:15? *"To one he gave five talents of money, to another two talents, and to another one talent, each according to his ability."* God gives to each of us according to our ability, and you can determine your ability.

God gives ability with an expectation that you will increase your ability. Have you ever increased your ability? It's very simple. Just get to work; get more education; learn from a master; gain more knowledge; gain more expertise. And of course, make some mistakes along the way. Eventually, you'll learn how to do it right. When you increase your ability, you profit more with that ability.

I believe the Church has gotten off track because we have created these four walls and said that's where the gifts of the Spirit should be used. Let's look again at Romans 12:4-6:

> *Just as each of us has one body with many members, as these members do not all have the same function, so in Christ we who are many form one body. Each member belongs to all the others. We have different gifts according to the grace given to us. If a man's gift is prophesying, let him use it in proportion to his faith.*

It does not say that the gift of prophecy should happen only in the church building. It does not confine its use to Saturday or Sunday in a building built for and used by Bible college graduates.

Let's continue reading Romans 12:

> *If it is serving, let him serve; if it is teaching, let him teach; if it is encouraging, let him encourage; if it is contributing to the needs of others, let him give generously; if it is leadership, let him govern diligently; if it is showing mercy, let him do it cheerfully* (Romans 12:7-8).

Again, it does not say "in the church." There's not even a footnote or a scholar somewhere who wrote an addendum at the bottom of the page that said, "This is only for the church." The church, according to the Bible, is a people, a congregation—not a group of people in a church building. Man has changed the meaning of the

word and misinterprets constantly what God is saying just by changing the meaning of *the church*. The gifts are to be used everywhere.
Let's keep going.

First Corinthians 12:8 says, *"To one there is given through the Spirit
the message of wisdom...."* The gifts are given through the Spirit, not
through the church building. They're the gifts of the *Spirit*. You get
them from God, not from people. You don't have to apply to the
church board for approval. You can have that message of wisdom.
Just ask God for the gifts of His Spirit. Acts 2 says to repent and be
baptized and you will be filled with the Holy Spirit.

You get the point. We are all eligible if we love God. Some of us
are kings, some are priests. We work at different places, but we have
the same Holy Spirit.

Unfortunately, situations and stories are too often twisted to put
the focus on the four walls of the church building. We have been
taught that that is where true ministry and the most important things
happen. We have believed that the Church is a building rather than
a people. And if the enemy can keep our thinking inside of the four
walls, we are not a threat to the kingdom of darkness.

If we can be tricked into believing that we have to serve only
in the church, contribute only in the church, prophesy only in the
church, and learn only in the church, then the enemy does not have
to fear us. The message has been twisted by hell. If we can only use
the gifts once we are super high up in the corporate structure of the
church and if we can only use the gifts in the building, then satan
has found a perfect plan to make sure that 90 percent of the Body of
Christ is irrelevant.

It doesn't say that those gifts are intended for within the four
walls. It also doesn't say that they're only for those in Bible college. It
only says that they're given by one Spirit. It also says that they're given
"just as He determines" (1 Cor. 12:11). God doesn't limit where we

use the gifts. There are no boundaries. We have a boundless God who works all these gifts for the edification of the Body of Christ.

Colossians 3:23 says, *"Whatever you do, work at it with all your heart, as working for the Lord, not for men."* Consider the words *whatever* and *everything*. They are nice, generic terms that include business, parenting, marriage, ministry, schoolwork, your profession, your trade. It says *whatever*. And as I've pointed out before, it doesn't say that this only applies in the church. It doesn't say in ministry. Your ministry is whatever you do as unto Him. I do everything as unto the Lord because it glorifies Him and it blesses people. That means that everything I do is ministry.

## DIVERSITY IS GOOD

As mentioned previously, Romans 12:4-5 says, *"Just as each of us has one body with many members and these members do not all have the same function, so in Christ we who are many form one body, and each member belongs to all the others."* This is so important that it bears repeating. Man's idea of unity is everybody looking, acting, walking, talking, and dressing the same. That is an ignorant, foolish philosophy because man's idea of unity is conformity, and conformity is a disease.

However, God's idea of unity is simple to figure out. Nothing is the same on this planet. Our DNA is different, our thumb prints are different, and the hairs on our heads are different. Grains of sand, shoots of grass, nothing at all on this planet was created exactly the same. Even identical twins are not the same.

God's idea of unity is diversity in harmony. We just read it. *"And these members do not all have the same function"* (Rom. 12:4). I'm not supposed to be the same as everybody else, and neither are you!

Have you felt that you are different from everybody else? Perhaps you've even been told that you're different from everybody else. It's almost like a putdown, but the reality is, it was by design that you're not like everybody else. The people who try to put you in a box just don't get it.

You can look everywhere and nothing's the same. I can't find two pairs of jeans that are the same. I can't get two meals in the same restaurant that are exactly the same. Have you come across people who have tried to change you? Have you had people in your church, whatever religion you serve, try to change you? You will be set free because I'm done with this nonsense. I'm done with it happening to me. I'm done with it happening to others.

> *We have different gifts according to the grace given to us. If a man's gift is prophesying, let him use it in proportion to his faith. If it is serving, let him serve. If it is teaching, let him teach. If it is in encouraging, let him encourage. If it is contributing to the needs of others, let him give generously. If it is leadership, let him govern diligently. If it is showing mercy, let him do it cheerfully* (Romans 12:6-8).

Ephesians 4:11-13 says:

> *It was He who gave some to be apostles, some to be prophets, some to be evangelists, some to be pastors and teachers to prepare God's people for works of service so that the body of Christ may be built up until we all reach unity in the faith and knowledge of the Son of God and become mature, attaining the whole measure in the fullness of Christ Jesus.*

Now, please don't get me wrong. I am not bashing the Church. I go to church. Every Sunday that I'm in town, I'm sitting in a house of worship. However, I will say that it was created by people and people's ideals. I believe we are a bit off track. We've turned church into a place, what I call a brick factory. We've made it cookie cutter—"If you're going to be spiritual, this is how you will act. If you're going to be spiritual, this is how you will dress."

## KINGLY ANOINTING

David was not a priest. He killed many people in battle; it was one of his primary vocational activities. Yet he was the apple of God's eye. He was anointed king at the age of 16, but it was many more years before he became king on the throne. When he was first anointed king, he had to serve a wicked, stupid, immature, impatient king named Saul, but David refused to dishonor him. He submitted to the headship, and he honored that king wholeheartedly. David could have spoke against him but he refused. Yet Christians speak against and gossip about their bosses or management and then expect God to prosper them. He won't—it's against His Word.

God tested David and trained him, in his youthful days, on how to rule. His first submission was to a king who he did not agree with. God knew that if this young man could submit to someone whom he did not agree with, he'd have to instead honor him. God knew that David would honor Him.

His first test was to see how David would respond to a king who had integrity issues as well as many other problems. David honored and submitted to this king, which meant he passed the test. If David could submit to the a king with major issues, then David could certainly be trusted to honor and submit to the King of all creation, Almighty God. David had every right to dishonor King Saul; however, he refused to do so. This showed that David was a man of honor and could be trusted with his own kingdom someday.

"He inquired of the Lord..." is said of David so many times in First and Second Samuel, it's unbelievable." In Psalms, we see David whining; we see him rejoicing. He cried out to God for absolutely everything. He cried out to God for marriage advice, kid advice, wars, battles, strategies, finances, and political issues. He inquired of the Lord on every step he took; he sought God in everything he did.

Every time he sought God, God gave his enemies into his hands. Do you have any enemies? Are you trying to fight them on your own? If God can take a 16-year-old who could single-handedly kill a bear and a lion and even a giant, why in the world are you trying to do it by yourself? That is stupidity. You're not supposed to.

You may have been taught that God doesn't have time for you, that you're not supposed to seek Him for those little battles, that you can handle it on your own. I'm sorry. David asked for absolutely everything. *God, what do you think? Should I attack now, or should I wait? Should I go yonder? Should I go to the west, or should I start in the east? What do you think I should do?* God would show him exactly what he was supposed to do, and his enemies would be defeated.

He shows us what the kingly anointing (the marketplace anointing) is all about. And he shows us that it is just as "spiritual" as the priestly (pastoral) anointing.

## NO SCHOOLING REQUIRED

I was in Belize not too long ago and the Lord brought an 18-year-old young man across our path. He spent the entire day with us. He makes great money; he just bought his first house and a condo in Belize. He was blown away by my children. And he started to ask questions. I said, "God has really blessed us." He looked at me cross-eyed, like he had never heard that before. Long story short, by the end of the evening, he got saved. I told him that just the week before I had been with one of my best friends who had gotten saved and had been baptized in my pool just a few days after. And he says to me, "You baptize people?" I said, "Dude, anyone can baptize people. John the Baptist didn't go to seminary to learn how to baptize. They didn't have it back then." The young man was like, "Oh, well baptize me." To which I replied, "Sure. Ocean or pool?"

At midnight, on July 4th, I baptized him in the ocean. He was baptized in the water, and all of a sudden, he asked me, "OK, when can I be baptized in the Holy Spirit?" So I told him about getting baptized in the Holy Spirit right then and there. He said, "Really?" I told him "Yea, just say this." He started to say it, and all of a sudden he was hit by the power of God, and his head went back, and it seemed like he was drowning.

God is my witness; my daughter Arika is my witness. He asked "What happened? I feel like a new person." I told him, "You are; you are, dude!" with tears running down my face.

Anybody can baptize anybody. We have turned this into a religious act with a corporate structure. We've made it that you have to graduate and take this test and do all this kind of stuff.

John the Baptist, under current, modern-day rules and regulations, would have been shot. Of course, they cut his head off back then, too. He didn't fit the mold. He didn't dress right, he didn't talk right, and he didn't act right. He did not know the right people. He did not come from that fandangle fancy church. He did not have a certificate of ordination. They would have slaughtered him in today's society, under today's rules and regulations. They would have called him a false prophet, slandered him, and belittled his credibility, ignoring his anointing.

He ate bugs. He was a full-on tree-hugger, a naturalist, a vegan. He was a homeless man, for goodness' sake. Not only that, he did not tell them what they wanted to hear, but he told them what they needed to hear. He told them to repent, walk away from their wicked ways, and prepare the way for the coming Lord. They responded by cutting off his head (see Matt. 3:1-10; 14:1-12).

The truth is that we have fallen asleep. The truth is, millions of drops of innocent blood are being shed right here in this nation every year. Our religious leaders walk in competition and jealousy. We, too, harbor judgment and jealousy. While we're fighting over our stupid, little doctrinal issues, innocent blood is being shed. Government has gone awry, and wickedness is all over the land.

Where are the Isaiahs? Where are the Jeremiahs? Where are the John the Baptists? Where are the Micahs, those who are not afraid to say, "We have screwed up and sinned against God"? We need to humble ourselves and pray. We need to do something about this, and it's time for us to repent.

But too often, we don't do that; instead, we have lots of fluffy words. We say, God's going to do this and God's going to do that. Those things are great, but until we repent, God isn't going to do anything. You go and read that whole Bible. The bottom line is that until we turn our hearts wholly to Him and we repent for our actions, we aren't going anywhere (see 2 Chron. 7:14).

Joseph was not a traditional minister. I don't know what it is, but whenever God's message is preached, it's preached in a way that puts the "old greats" of faith in the box of traditional ministry within the traditional four walls.

Joseph was a businessman. We have created idols in our Bibles that are false. They were marketplace people who rose up in their calling in the marketplace. There was no church. Joseph was a little shepherd boy, the least in his family. His brothers hated him. He was full of pride. He would say, "God gave me a vision. You're the loser. I'm going to win." God had to discipline him.

Joseph had a vision that he knew was going to happen. But he told it to the wrong people. Moral of the story: Don't cast your pearls before swine (see Matt. 7:6). His brothers turned against him. They threw him in a pit and sold him into slavery. He was brought to Egypt as a slave, but he prospered. He used his abilities, and he prospered from them. He learned skills. He learned laboring skills. He learned construction skills. He learned how to become a foreman.

He applied himself to everything he learned. He got better. He applied the ability; God gave him more ability. Then he was promoted up to the governor's house. He learned in his house business skills, money management skills, people skills, leadership skills, real estate skills. He was being groomed by the governor. Joseph had this dream, and he thought that it meant that he was going to lead his little tribe. But God had something else in mind.

Most people are waiting for some supernatural way to learn a new skill. God has people in front of you from whom you are supposed to be learning. Most people have loads of chances to put themselves into positions to learn from others who are successful financially, in careers, family, and so on, but because they are looking for some supernatural nugget to fall out of the sky, they miss the obvious supernatural direction of God. Joseph took advantage of learning from everyone around him.

So in the midst of slavery, in the midst of bondage, Joseph was falsely accused and sent to prison. But even in prison he prospered. He took the business administrator skills he had learned in the governor's house and applied them in the prison. He gained more abilities, more favor, and eventually was promoted from a slave to a ruler.

So Joseph's interpretation of the dream was actually smaller than the real meaning. And he received his training for ministry in slavery and prison. He had no formal ministry training, but he knew God and loved God and honored God with his gifts. This put him in a position to change and preserve several nations.

So if you've been deceived into thinking that you are worthless or useless in the Body of Christ, its time to step into truth and use what you have been given to advance the Kingdom of Heaven. Just as God used people in the Bible who had no formal training in ministry to do some amazing things for history, He can also use you. It's time to step up and use all you've got for the Kingdom of Heaven.

*At the Spiritual Equipping Service I opened my heart to what you had to say, and I received great words of wisdom that I can apply to my life and my business. Thank you for taking the time and effort to share your heart and faith with us.*

—Craig U

## CHAPTER 7

# DISCOVERING YOUR GIFTS

Let's return to Romans 12 and First Corinthians 12, which between them list 15 gifts of the Spirit:

*We have different gifts, according to the grace given us. If a man's gift is prophesying, let him use it in proportion to his faith. If it is serving, let him serve; if it is teaching, let him teach; if it is encouraging, let him encourage; if it is contributing to the needs of others, let him give generously; if it is leadership, let him govern diligently; if it is showing mercy, let him do it cheerfully* (Romans 12:6-8).

*To one there is given through the Spirit the message of wisdom, to another the message of knowledge by means of the same Spirit, to another faith by the same Spirit, to another gifts of healing by that one Spirit, to another miraculous powers, to another prophecy, to another distinguishing between spirits, to another speaking in different kinds of tongues, and to still another the interpretation of tongues* (1 Corinthians 12:8-10).

We're going to look at all 15 gifts that the Bible says are given by the same Spirit. In this chapter, you're going to discover your gifts and the gifts of other people. You're going to learn how you can use these gifts and how they work in the marketplace.

## PROPHECY

The gift of prophecy is written about throughout the Bible, from Genesis through Revelation. I strongly urge you to read the Bible cover to cover so you may see with your own eyes how God works, those He works through, and how He operates and what provokes His mercy as well as His wrath.

The gift of prophecy seems to have multiple purposes. Many years ago in a tiny church in the mountains of California, a pastor gave the explanation of prophecy as to give exhortation, edification, and comfort. At the time I heard that definition I knew nothing about prophecy, and the simplicity of that definition started me on a path to study it further.

The Bible doesn't come out and say "the gift of prophecy is...," no not at all actually. However, if you read the Bible cover to cover the Holy Spirit begins to open your eyes as you read the prophetic words and you gain revelation about the gift. As I studied I did find that prophecy definitely did give *exhortation, edification,* and *comfort*—as well as a few other things.

Let's follow the trail of what those words mean in order to flesh out *prophecy* a bit further. *Exhortation* means "to urge strongly, earnestly, persuade." Many attorneys have the gift of prophecy. And they don't even know it. Have you ever noticed that attorneys paint pictures with their words? They have a gift of persuasion. The gift of persuasion falls underneath the gift of prophecy. Are you good at persuading? That is a gift from Heaven.

*Edification* means "to improve, enlighten, and bring guidance." Do you do that in your profession? A lot of teachers have a gift of prophecy. Prophecy is forth-telling, speaking it out. Often, people who are prophetic see visions or pictures and they have dreams, and then those things happen.

*Comfort* means consolation; relief in affliction; solace, cheer, ease, soothe. Are you one of those individuals who operate in the comforting of others? That is actually the Holy Spirit working in you, and it is the Holy Spirit who gives the gift of prophecy by His Spirit. So when you are comforting someone you are operating in the gift of prophecy. The gift without training leads to destruction. When you don't know that you have the gift of prophecy, who gave you the gift, and what you're supposed to do with it, you will use it for the wrong reasons.

Throughout the Bible we see many other ways prophecy is demonstrated for other reasons as well. For example, we see prophecy being used to strengthen. The word *strengthen* means "to reinforce, renew, bolster, fortify, confirm, intensify, invigorate, nourish, and rejuvenate." Elijah is a perfect example of running in fear after his greatest victory and the Lord sending a bird to nourish him back to strength—to speak life into a dead situation. Also, there is Gideon and the dead bones.

We also see prophecy used to encourage. The word *encourage* means "to give courage, to give confidence or hope, to reassure, inspire, urge, support, advance, promote." I have personally watched a word of encouragement bring people and situations to life just as it is shown in the Bible. Someone who speaks with encouraging words is absolutely operating in a gift of prophecy. We see even in Numbers 22 when Balak is trying to hire Balaam to prophesy negatively against Israel. Balak was not an Israelite, and yet he knew the power of prophecy as well as Balaam, who also was not an Israelite prophet. In fact, in that same story, God spoke thru Balaam's donkey. Read the story; it's hilarious. Listen, if God will speak through a donkey, he can certainly speak through you, and you can begin utilizing the gift through speaking encouraging words over people and situations.

*Warning* is also used quite often in prophecy. Warning means "to caution, admonish, advise, counsel." We do this very often with our kids or loved ones if we see them doing something that is hurtful to their future. Warning and encouragement is a form of prophecy as well (see 2 Chron. 15). Other prophetic words of warning include correction, such as with Nathan after David's sin with Bathsheba in Second Samuel 12. Direction is given in Genesis 16 with Hagar being told to return to her mistress. There are warnings all through Jeremiah and Ezekiel. There are also prophetic words of promotion, as in David being anointed king long before he received the throne.

There are prophetic words of warning to build faith, as in Joshua 1, and a call to repentance and forthtelling in Luke 3 with John the Baptist. According to Revelation 19:10, the testimony of Jesus is the spirit of prophecy; so every time you are telling people about Jesus, you are prophesying. If we really know Him, we can't help but tell everyone what He has done for us, whether it is in a restaurant bathroom (yes, I led a server to Christ in a bathroom stall in Dana Point, California), on an airplane (yes, I led a Jewish gal to Christ on an airplane; she was crying as she asked for forgiveness for denying Him as the Messiah), or in a bar (yes, I've led a man to Christ right in the middle of a bar, tears running down his face).

It doesn't matter where you are or who you are, at the minimum you want to prophesy and start telling people about Jesus. The spirit of prophecy automatically shows up and leads people to Him. Many operate in the gift of prophecy and simply don't know it or we think only the super special ones have the gift. How special is a donkey? I think you're qualified. It's time to step out and use the gift, and as you do you will receive more because, according to Romans 12, we prophecy according to the measure of faith that we have. The more you use it, the more you get. So get on with it.

Have you ever had that happen to you? Have you ever had a hunch about something and all of a sudden it happened. Have you ever driven by an area, sensed that an accident is about to happen, and right before your eyes there it is? That's a gift of prophecy. The Bible says to use the gift of prophecy in proportion to your faith (see Rom. 12:6). Ask for a greater measure of faith.

## SERVICE

The second gift is serving. Are you a nurse? You have the gift to serve. Are you in the food service business? You have a gift to serve. It probably comes naturally to you. Where there is a need, you have a natural desire to fill the need. If something needs to be done, you have a natural desire to do it. "I'll take care of that. I'd be glad to." And you actually find satisfaction in helping other people. Is that you? That's a gift from the Holy Spirit.

## TEACHING

Teaching is the next gift. It applies to teaching anything. It does not say that it only involves teaching the Word of God. It's a gift from God no matter what the subject matter. Do you love to teach? That is a gift and a calling from God. You probably can't help yourself. You start teaching others in the middle of conversations. It's just who you are. Teaching is a high call. You are passing on wisdom, knowledge, and experience that you've gained. You're passing it down to one who is unlearned and helping them to increase their abilities.

## ENCOURAGEMENT

The gift of encouragement can be used in calling out the destiny of someone else or even yourself. King David encouraged his own self and told his own soul not to be downcast:

> *Why are you downcast, O my soul?*
> *Why so disturbed within me? Put your hope in God,*
> *for I will yet praise Him, my Savior and my God.*
> *My soul is downcast within me; therefore I will*
> *remember you from the land of the Jordan, the*
> *heights of Hermon—from Mount Mizar*
> (Psalm 42:5-6).

Do you, for some reason, see good in people? Do you, for some reason, see good in bad situations? If so, that's a spiritual gift of encouragement. Paul said, "If it [the gift] is encouraging, let him encourage…" (Rom. 12:8). This doesn't just apply to the time you spend in a church building. You're called to be an encourager everywhere and in everything you do. At the grocery store, in a restaurant, at work, use this gift to encourage the world. In my professional opinion, people rarely get encouragement from anyone. You will stand out like a light on a hill if you encourage everyone around you.

## CONTRIBUTING TO THE NEEDS OF OTHERS

Contributing to the needs of others, or giving, is a spiritual gift. The Bible says, *"Let him give generously"* (Rom. 12:8). Why is it that so many people put down making money? The Bible says that giving money is a spiritual gift. That means that you have to have money to contribute first. If you don't have any money, you can't contribute it.

Some people who contribute are put down because they "only" contribute money. "Well, fine. You just give money, but where are you serving?" This should not be. Giving and serving are both gifts of the Spirit, and one is not better than the other.

My husband felt like a bad Christian his whole Christian walk because he was money motivated. Every time there was a call for volunteers, he was like, "I don't want to do that." He had no desire to help at all in any of their functions, and he felt condemned because of it. Finally one day he said, "You know what, God? This is the way You made me, so You're going to have to deal with me. If You want me to change, then change me."

God didn't change him. God stirred him even stronger to make more money. He even had him focus on learning new skills in computers, programming, and understanding marketing. When he was freed from the shame that had been put on him through condemnation, he finally started seeking out and increasing his skills.

Then the Lord gave him a revelation. His calling is to make a lot of money. He's called us to make a lot of money so that we can give it away to people who are in need. We give it away to the people that want to love on the babies in Africa. We give it away to people who have orphanages here in the United States for abused children. We are able to give millions of dollars to those in need.

Thank God that my husband was set free; otherwise he'd still be a boring, unusable man of God, who actually would be called a wicked, lazy servant because his gift was not released. Now his goal is to give away $1 million a month.

If more Christians were no longer wrongly judged and even condemned for making money but instead understood the Bible and the purpose for money, I believe that billions would go to contributing to the needs of others, and it would change the world. Christians would also have more influence because we live in a world where money talks and you know what walks. I recently heard that Christians give to missions as much as Americans spend on dog food. Ouch!

## LEADERSHIP

The Bible says of the one with a gift of leadership, *"Let him govern diligently"* (Rom. 12:8). I don't know what it is, but the people who have the gift of leadership just seem to rise up. Joseph rose up; David rose up. Is that you? No matter where you go or what you do, do you seem to rise up? Of course, as we all know by now, it does not say you must lead as a church leader.

It says, *"If it [the gift] is leadership, let him govern diligently"* (Rom. 12:8). Leadership was designed and given to happen everywhere, not just in church. Do you have a gift of influence, a gift of leadership? Do you always seem to wind up in leadership roles? That's a gift from God. The world needs leaders like you.

## MERCY

The seventh gift is mercy. The Word of God says, *"Let him do it cheerfully "* (Rom. 12:8). Do you have a heart for the hurting? Do you have a heart for the needy? When people are hurting, do you hurt with them? Will you do anything to rescue or help another? Will you lay down your life for somebody else? That's a gift of mercy. If you're as compassionate as I am, you have the gift of mercy. Do you want to see restoration? Do you want to see redemption? Do you want to see reconciliation? Do you want to see families healed? That's a gift of mercy.

## MESSAGE OF WISDOM

First Corinthians 12:8 says, *"To one there is given through the Spirit the message of wisdom...."* Has this ever happened to you? You don't know where it comes from, but all of a sudden you open your mouth and something smart flies out. You say, "That was really cool. Where'd that come from?" That is the Spirit of the Most High God. You open your mouth, words come out, and you're like, *That was good. I have to write that down.*

Does that ever happen to you? That's the Spirit of the Lord coming on you, giving you a message of wisdom. Have you had that happen and people tell you to shut up? Have you had that happen to you and people reject the message? I have, but the message isn't mine; it comes from above.

A lot of accountants have the gift of wisdom. Analysts and engineers also have this gift. Have you ever seen these people operate? My husband has a monster gift of wisdom. It's amazing. We say in our office that Hans has seven brains because there's no way that much could fit into one head. All the different dimensions that he thinks in are unbelievable. Does this sound like you? It's a gift of wisdom. God gave you a different brain, and it's amazing.

## MESSAGE OF KNOWLEDGE

A lot of counselors operate in the gift of knowledge. This is how the gift of knowledge works. If you have the gift of knowledge, you may receive understanding about someone's past. It's knowledge that you do not know in the natural. It's called a word of knowledge. God gives you a download about another person.

You probably don't know that person; you don't know anything about them. For some reason, you see something. Their face speaks something to you. God shows you what's going on in their heart, with their desires, and so forth. When you share it with them, they usually say, "How did you know that?"

I experienced something similar in Australia. I met a guy, and I asked him, "Do you drive a red car?" He said, "Yeah." I didn't know the guy at all. I'd never met him before; I don't know if I'll ever see him again. He asked me, "How did you know that?" I then proceeded to give him a message from God, and it was dead on. That's what is called a word of knowledge.

Has that every happened to you before? That's the Spirit of the Most High God coming on you to deliver a message, a word of knowledge. But if you don't know that you have the gift, you won't use it.

## FAITH

Faith is risk taking. Faith is being obedient to a vision. Faith is answering a call. Faith is stepping out with no guarantee. Faith is believing whole-heartedly in the unseen. Faith is having the impression and urge of promise and then eagerly stepping out toward it, even if it doesn't make any sense, even if it doesn't look like it's going to work.

God makes a way where there is no way. He uses the foolish things to confound the wise (see 1 Cor. 1:27). The Bible says, *"The Lord will make you the head, not the tail....You will always be at the top, never at the bottom"* (Deut. 28:13). We are above and not beneath. He makes crooked ways straight for us. It takes the gift of faith to believe and act on all of this.

Today Abraham would be considered a nutcase by most Christians because he heard voices: "Leave your father's house." He and his dad were rich men. He had servants, cows, and sheep. He was very wealthy. But he obeyed and left anyway, and everything started dying. The sheep were dying, the babies were dying, the women were dying, and the men were dying. The crops failed, and famine was in the land (see Gen. 12:10). But Abraham kept following God's word. His faith was in the unseen.

God said to Abraham, *"I will surely bless you and make your descendants as numerous as the stars in the sky and as the sand on the seashore…"* (Gen. 22:17).

It says in Romans 4:9 that *"Abraham's faith was credited to him as righteousness."* So when you step out in faith to build your business, career, investments, when you step out in faith to speak what is unseen, when you step out in faith to walk as though it is already, it is attributed to you as righteousness. That's faith. There is no faith in something that's comfortable or easy. There is no faith in something that's normal or the status quo. That is not faith.

Are you an entrepreneur? You have the gift of faith. If you have stepped out and borrowed money to invest in a project, that is a gift of faith. If you have stepped out to find some investors who will believe in your project, that is the gift of faith. Have you stepped out and done really stupid things with no guarantee? It's credited to you as righteousness. That doesn't apply to all the stupid things you've done, but to some of them—the ones that were inspired by faith in God. That is the gift of faith.

## HEALING

Healings happen in many different ways. When the Lord gave me this revelation years ago, I crumbled. I absolutely crumbled and repented on behalf of our entire nation for this one.

For some reason, certain sects of the Church define healing only in terms of a divine touch from Heaven. They don't count what happened with Hezekiah. King Hezekiah was sent to a doctor. A doctor came, gave him a prescription that healed him, and he lived 15 more years (see 2 Kings 20:1-7). In this nation, we've glorified our doctors, rather than God, by saying that they have healed us. God is always the one who heals, even when He uses doctors.

People often see it as failure if they have cancer and have to go through chemotherapy to get better. They think God didn't heal them. But He did. God uses different ways to heal. It's shown throughout the entire Bible. Yet we want to give the doctor the glory when it takes surgery for someone to be healed. The doctor gets the glory if it's chemo. I fell on the floor in my office, crying out to God saying, "Lord God, please forgive me on behalf of our whole nation, which has exalted the ones whom You've given the gift of healing to instead of glorifying You, the Healer."

If you have been healed by using modern-day drugs, consider who inspired the scientists who invented the drugs. Do you think they just pulled the formula out of nowhere? These scientists had a word from the Lord. It doesn't matter if they don't give God credit for it. The bottom line is, God inspired, gave wisdom, and gave knowledge to invent medicines and machines. So there are divine healings and there are physical healings, or healings through concoction or diet. And God Almighty is the author and finisher of all of it.

Have you ever been healed? Have you been divinely healed? Have you had a touch from God and the sickness or the disease was gone? I have! I have medical documentation of a fatal heart condition. The side effect of it was sudden death, which meant that no one would be able to get to me fast enough to resuscitate me. I have a doctor's note that said I couldn't fly, that I couldn't be in high elevation. I used to pass out three or four times a day. The Lord healed my body, and now I travel in airplanes every few weeks. I no longer pass out, and I take no medications at all.

Even more exciting is the story of Kimberly, a single mom who came to my seminar in Chicago, Illinois. The Lord had me pull her out of the audience, lay hands on her, and bind up a spirit of death. Little did I know that she was dying of cancer. But she was completely healed that night. She went home, and after a year of business failure, she was able to make $10,000 in three weeks. And she led her seven-year-old son to Christ. She came back to a seminar a year later and said that she's cancer free. She screamed out, "I am still alive!" And she paid off $32,000 in debt in one year. Every ounce of that story is a miracle. Use your business or career to pray for the sick. God will shock you and heal them. He has shocked me now thousands of times. Do you have a desire to see the sick healed, set free, and delivered? Who do you think put that desire in you? God did, and He did it because you are to lay hands on the sick and you will see them healed.

## MIRACULOUS POWERS

You may have been taught that miraculous powers don't happen today; if that's your case, that's tragic. In my hometown I met a woman who, for 38 years, when she opens up her Bible in a worship service, manna comes from Heaven and lands on her Bible. I have a piece of it in my wallet. I ate some. It tastes pretty good.

Miracles include things like feathers falling out of nowhere and gold dust appearing on people's faces. We had a man in our meetings who did not believe in God and whose leg grew right before his wife's eyes. This didn't happen at a church service or some Christian conference, it happened at a seminar in the marketplace where people where coming to learn how to get wealthy. Miracles in the marketplace happen the same way Jesus did it. Do you want the anointing? Step out in faith in the marketplace; people are waiting just as when Jesus was there.

As you can imagine, he now believes in God. It happened. This man testified, right before his wife, with tears running down his face. He said, "My leg grew." That is called a miracle. If for some reason you believe that you have to be that very super-spiritual evangelist with the powerful anointing who has received an anointing from some other super-spiritual evangelist, try this one on for size. What about the witch from Endor, written about in First Samuel 28? Check it out. It will shock you. She had some pretty powerful miraculous powers. A witch—how qualified and holy and righteous and pure was she? This witch called up Samuel from the dead to speak to Saul. It's the enemy of your soul who wants you to think that all of these harder, crazier gifts are not for you. Because if you think that they are not for you, you certainly will not seek God to be used by His Spirit for the good of His people.

## DISCERNING OF SPIRITS

The next gift is the gift of discerning of spirits. Do you have a lie-o-meter? (You know when someone is lying to you.) That is an inexperienced version of discernment. You need a better, advanced version of the gift of discernment. Such a gift helps you distinguish between spirits, between God and the devil, so that you know who is talking to you.

## SPEAKING IN DIFFERENT TONGUES

You may not believe in this, but the Bible clearly talks about speaking in a language that you do not know, that you have not learned (see 1 Cor. 12:10). All I know is that people who didn't even believe in speaking in other tongues now have the gift of tongues. At a recent business seminar that I was teaching in Los Angeles, a woman by the name of Gerri told her story:

In March of this year, it was at the end of prayer, and we were standing in the back praying for people, and I was behind a woman. I think I put my hands on her, and I just started speaking in tongues. And I went, "Oh my gosh. What is going on?" I just thought it was the weirdest thing. I never wanted that gift. I never asked for that gift. God blessed me with that gift, and I've been using it ever since. I don't know how to explain it. All I know is it happens.

He who speaks in an unknown tongue does not speak to man but speaks to God (see 1 Cor. 14:2).

## INTERPRETATION OF TONGUES

The gift of interpretation is when you hear somebody speaking in tongues, and all of a sudden, you understand what they are saying, and you interpret it. That's trippy.

## TRAIN YOUR GIFT

I want you to seriously consider what I am about to say. The gifts of God are irrevocable (see Rom. 11:29). Either you will use yours for yourself, for the enemy, or for God. Only if you use it for God will it have long-lasting fruit. Not only that, but it will also be eternal instead of just temporary.

Once we know what our gifts are, we must do all we can to develop them. The gifts without training lead to destruction. The gifts are given to us by the Spirit. And the gifts will be made complete by the Spirit, which means that you have to spend time with the Spirit. The gifts are not for your glory, but for His. They are for equipping the saints, for equipping people, not a building (see Eph. 4:11-13). They're for building the Kingdom of Heaven, not just a "bricks-and-mortar" building.

I have seen all of these gifts activated in the marketplace, *all of them!* I have not, however, seen all of them activated in the vast majority of churches. This is sad. Just as the Scripture says He has given them to all men, it's up to us to activate them by using them. Step out in faith and begin to use what you have already received by the

Spirit. God will meet you there, and you will be shocked to see what happens. You may also be scared, as I was scared.

The first time I did an altar call for my clients to receive Christ was sooooo scary. I thought my clients were going to stone me, boo me, hate me, and write nasty letters. I was shocked when 85 percent of the people in the room came running to the stage. Hindus, atheists, Buddhists, Muslims, you name it, they came to receive Jesus of Nazareth. There were healings, prophetic words, and several even received the gift of tongues that night—in a secular seminar with people from all over the world. Our clients were there to learn how to increase their wealth, manage their time, and improve their relationships. Those in sales or business were there to radically grow their sales—they got all that, and Jesus too! Their lives were changed.

*Thank you for the Spiritual Equipping Session. What Christ has done through you has changed our lives forever. I'll never look at business or relationships the same way again!*

—ANGELA F

CHAPTER 8

# CREATING UNITY IN A DIVERSE CULTURE

The enemy has a plan to divide and conquer God's people. He wants you to think that you have nothing to offer the King of kings and the Lord of lords. He wants to make you think that what you have is not useful for anybody else. Here are four ways, which I discovered through my own experience, that the enemy tries to divide and conquer:

1. **We become jealous of other people's gifts.** We are judgmental toward others and belittle other people's gifts. We tear them apart because we do

not realize that we *do* have gifts and that we're not using them. With jealousy and judgment in our hearts we are deceived into coveting other people's gifts not realizing that we have our own and they are more perfect for us than someone else's. In this deception our time is not spent in developing our own gifts.

2.    **We don't use our gifts.** The one who doesn't use his talent is considered a wicked, lazy servant (see Matt. 25:26-30). Those who receive an ability from God and do not use their gift, according to the Word of God, are wicked, lazy servants.

3.    **We abuse our gifts because of ignorance.** If we do not know that our gifts are from God, we will abuse them and use them for the wrong reasons. We will use them to glorify ourselves instead of God, and we will exalt ourselves instead of exalting God and others.

4.    **We feel useless and worthless.** We feel that our lives are a waste of time and that we are isolated and alone.

You should know by now that you are being used by God, even when you don't know it. What a loving God. We need to work together and not put each other down. We don't need to try to change each other. We're all different parts of one Body. We can't survive without each other's gifts (see 1 Cor. 12:12-26). It's time that we recognize our gifts and use them to the fullest while accepting and embracing other people's gifts and cheering them on.

What we have done is put walls in the Body of Christ. The Bible says that the Body of Christ is us (see Rom. 12:5; 1 Cor. 12:12; Col. 3:15). We represent the Body. The Body of Christ, the Church, is not a building with walls. It is wall-less. And those of us who are in Christ represent Christ—we are the Church. That's who we are.

You may have been taught, like me (in good-heartedness but ignorance) that the gifts of God are only given to super-spiritual people who belong to the right church. Let's think about this. Who in the world would want you to believe that you are not special and that you cannot use all of your gifts? Who would want you to think that you have no access to miraculous powers, prophecy, healing, tongues, interpretation of tongues, wisdom, or knowledge?

The destroyer, the devil who was defeated 2,000 years ago, has a lying mouth, and he'll do all he can to keep you inactive in the Kingdom (see John 8:44). If he can get you to believe that you don't have access to the gifts of the spirit, you certainly won't use them. And if you don't use them, you're not a threat to the kingdom of darkness.

Ephesians 4:11 says:

> *It was He who gave some to be apostles, some to be prophets, some to be evangelists, and some to be pastors and teachers, to prepare God's people for works of service so that the body of Christ may be built up until we reach unity in the faith and in the knowledge of the Son of God and become mature, attaining to the whole measure of the fullness of Christ.*

## THE FIVE POSITIONS

In the last chapter, we defined each of the gifts of the Spirit. What we didn't do is define the positions: apostle, prophet, evangelist, pastor, and teacher. We're going to define those in this next section with the object of showing you how to create unity in a diverse culture.

## Apostle

Ephesians 4:11 says *"It was He who gave some to be apostles."* Let's talk about what that looks like. I'm going to tell you what that means in layman terms. The text doesn't say evangelists in the church, apostles in seminary, or prophets in a four-walled building. It does not say that. There are no walls, no boundaries at all. But somehow we have decided that those titles are only set for those in manmade traditional ministry as most know it.

Let me prove something to you. David was the apple of God's eye, and he was not a pastor. David didn't go to seminary. He was a warrior! The apple of God's eye was a warrior, a worshiper, and a king. John the Baptist was not a traditional minister, either. He didn't go to seminary to learn how to baptize or preach. Anyone who is in Christ can baptize or preach. But we have created these rules and regulations that do not exist in the Bible.

What is an apostle according to the Scriptures? An apostle is the head of an organization. An apostle can be someone who is a forerunner who starts something out of thin air, a leader who equips other leaders to lead. An apostle can also operate as an evangelist, prophet, pastor, and teacher with signs and wonders following.

Apostles can pastor, which means that they can nourish the people who are following them. They can feed them, protect them, and help to groom them. They can also teach; they can equip other people with new skills. Signs and wonders, according to the Bible, follow an apostle (see 2 Cor. 12:12).

A founder of a company, a forerunner who has a vision, tests the vision, collaborates with others, and brings people along to "dig the trenches" and make the vision happen. An apostle is even like a general contractor. Have you ever met a general contractor? Are you a general contractor? That's an apostolic anointing. A contractor is someone who can actually do all parts of that job. He sees a plot of dirt and says, "I see a building." He formulates the plans, hires the people, and pulls them all together to get the job done.

An apostle is a fire starter who goes into a situation, digs in the trench, starts with nothing, builds something, and then moves on to something else, leaving the people fully trained and able to carry on the work themselves. That's an apostolic anointing. This person duplicates himself wherever he goes. He is a leader who trains up other leaders.

### Prophet

Prophets are futuristic thinkers. They're doers, people who are speaking visions, speaking about the future, speaking where we're going to be some day. Do you know people like this? That's a prophetic gift. They're the ones who cast visions. They bring a fresh message; often they bring correction. They'll call you on your stuff. They also bring you to restoration.

Micah is a prime example of a biblical prophet. During his time, the priests were doing wrong. The king was doing wrong. And Micah was some no-name, nobody from nowhere, with nothing, who went up to the governmental authorities and said, "God is going to get you. You are taking bribes from the rich and you are not giving justice to the poor." That's what he said. "You are not doing things right, and if you do not repent and turn away from your wicked ways, God is going to punish you!"

He went to the king and said, "If you do not turn from your wicked ways, if you don't honor God, and you do not worship Him in the high places, then He is going to punish you bad!" That's Micah. The desire of a prophet is to bring people to restoration and reconciliation.

Is that you? Do you know people who are like that? They're not titled prophetess or prophet on their business card at such and such assemblies or whatever church. Many have the gift and don't know it because of the boundaries that we have put on the gift and the calling.

### Evangelist

This is someone who likes to get things done right *now*. They are results-oriented. They don't want it done next year or next week, but right now. They are always great promoters, always have people around them. They are great recruiters, great in sales, and they always make a flurry of things happen out of absolutely nowhere. They create chaos out of thin air.

An evangelist is obviously a person who's called into ministry. The evangelist comes winning souls for the Kingdom of Heaven. That's how it's exemplified, but the same exact gifts operate in those who work in sales. They want to promote; they want to rally. They're motivators. Do you know people like that? They have the gift of evangelism; they just don't know it.

### Pastor

Pastors are the ones who want to shepherd people. They have a flock; they have people that follow them. They want to nurture and protect. Someone in management sometimes can be a pastor. The heart of a pastor wants to create a safe place. They want to huddle and love on you. That's the way they are. You go to their house and they bring you a cup of tea and rub your back. They like to lead people into better, safer places for their lives to be improved. They are a bit gentler and have a softer approach than a prophet. If you follow the stories of the prophets in the Bible, you will see often a harsh approach in rebuking and correcting. John the Baptist in Luke 3 is a good example: "You brood of vipers...repent!"

### Teacher

A teacher has a very important job. God does not necessarily hold one higher than the other. A teacher's job is to equip the next generation. They teach others the vital things that have to be done. Without teachers, none of us would know how to read, write, add, or subtract. They pass on knowledge and wisdom. The Bible says that people perish for a lack of knowledge (see Hosea 4:6). They pass down to the next group tradition, wisdom, and knowledge, so that they can carry it through to the next generation following that.

Do you qualify in any of those five positions? Of course; all of us do. The unfortunate thing is that most people in these positions have not been trained how to deal with people, which is what their entire life and career is centered around. This is why we have so many people wounded and walking away from God. This is so important; it's why gifting without training leads to destruction.

## OPERATING IN UNITY

It is evident that we all have different functions. We all have different gifts. We all have different abilities. And along with all those differences, we also carry the different places that we've come from. We come from different states of mind, different points of view. This is why arguing happens; we all have our own personal points of view and our personal agendas about what we passionately feel is the right way to do things.

Unity is the only way that we can appreciate people's gifts and help them to explode with those gifts. However, in most cases people are stunting the gifts of others. They are stunting people's growth, which is neither fair nor right.

Because of all the different points of view that we have, because of all the different opinions that we have, an illustration using the United States military is helpful. Different branches specialize in different functions. We have the Navy, Air Force, Army, and Marines. The Navy watches over the water, the Air Force protects the skies, and the Marines are security. All of them have specific trained knowledge in specific areas. All of them have gifts by the same Spirit, so to speak.

So, we know that anything divided against itself will not stand (see Mark 3:25). This is why we need enough maturity to understand that everyone has different gifts. The key is, in business and any leadership role (ministry, family, etc.), to give a platform for the gifts to be exemplified. Leaders must make a place for the gifts to be groomed and edified. They need to provide a place where people can begin discovering and practicing their gifts instead of trapping them in a place they don't belong, such as the nursery for the person with an evangelistic gift.

## UNITY KILLERS

Here are three things that make it is impossible to have unity: jealousy, judgment, and pride.

### *Jealousy*

It's impossible to have unity with jealousy. It is absolutely impossible to have unity in an organization if jealousy is present. This includes jealousy of people's gifts, recognition, position, money, spouse, or happiness. If jealousy is present, unity cannot exist because jealousy causes division.

### *Judgment*

It is impossible to have unity with judgment. Judgment belittles someone else's gifts, position, or success. And nonacceptance of certain people (which happens because of judgment) causes division, not unity. When you won't listen, you're critical, and you have to be the chief authority on everything, you are walking in absolute judgment. You're exalting yourself.

## *Pride*

It's impossible to have unity where there is pride. Pride is essentially the belief that everything is set up to serve you. Prideful people must have the credit for everything, even for things that others do. They have to do everything themselves. They say, "Nobody else can do it better than me, so I'm the chief authority. Just sit down and shut up. I'll take care of all 25 of those things tomorrow." Prideful people think it's their job to change other people. But the only one any of us can change is ourselves. Instead of trying to change others, we need to change how we deal with the inadequacies and incompetence in other people.

I have watched countless times the pride of a leader purposely not give opportunity for someone's obvious gift. Unfortunately, most leaders are intimidated, and do what they can to keep the one on the rise shut down. They will have to answer to God for that. If you have been suppressed, don't worry about a thing, God will not let your gifts die in you as long as you are using them whenever possible. God will open doors that no man can shut. He has done it with me, He will do it for you.

## UNITY BUILDERS

Now let me show you the attitudes that are the glue for unity (in no particular order).

## *Love*

It is impossible to have unity in your marriage, family, business, and so forth, without love. Three kinds of love are necessary for unity. The first is love for the head or leader. For example, in my life, the head is my God and my husband, Hans. The head inside of our corporation is Hans.

The second kind of love is for one another—a brotherly love, a threefold cord that can't be easily broken (see Eccles. 4:12). This love allows us to cover each other and honor one another. The third kind of love is love for the vision, love for what the organization represents and stands for.

You need love for your leader, you need love for one another, and you need love for the vision. You should look for people who will love your vision and love the game. Have you ever noticed how much Olympic athletes love their game? It's powerful. That's what you're looking for in your family, ministry, and business—people who will love the game and love the vision. You're eventually going to teach them how to love the head who is God almighty.

### Acceptance

Acceptance is demonstrated in this way—mercy. Being merciful to one another, being there for one another, in times of trials and mistakes, is what unity is all about. If you want a unified organization, if you want a unified family, then you need to be one who covers other people's backs instead of kicking people when they're down. Instead of reminding them of their mistakes, you must remind them of the position that they're called to. You must remind them that you believe in them and show them mercy, even when it doesn't make any sense.

In Ephesians 2:4-5 it says that the Lord is gracious and compassionate, slow to anger and rich in love. All you have to do is read the Bible and you will see that this is true. He should have killed His own people a thousand times. And if it were me, I would have. They gave Him 400 years of total defilement, yet He sent His own Son to die for them (and us, because we're no better).

Acceptance is twofold. Not only is acceptance covering each other's backs, it is also receiving and embracing other's gifts without trying to change them to be like yours. Acceptance in an organization is so powerful, so huge. If you've ever been in a place that showed you these areas of acceptance, you know that it's a safe place to grow in. Anything is possible when people stand by you and say, "I love your gifts. Let's find a place where we can use them because I believe in your future and because I believe in the God who gave you the gifts. He has a plan and a future for them through you."

We all know that such an organization would be the most powerful place to be involved with. Rather than complaining about the lack of such places, go create one. I did with my companies. Create acceptance in your environment, and you will be amazed at the kind of production that you will see.

### Teamwork

Teamwork is the opportunity for all members to use their gifts for the benefit of the whole. Often leaders have a very big challenge with teamwork. A lot of leaders are single players. But they cannot build what's in their hearts by themselves. They cannot; they will not; they will crack. I don't care how great they think they are; they are not going to get to the top by themselves. It's just not going to happen. None of us can get to the top without the help of others' gifts, which in some areas are better than ours.

### Humility

Humility means thinking others higher than yourself (see Phil. 2:3). I have heard that preached so wrong it's pathetic. Thinking others higher than yourself is not putting yourself down. Thinking others higher than yourself doesn't mean that you squash yourself to make them feel better. That's called false humility. Humility is when you know you're nothing without God. You know only He can satisfy. You know you only have because He has given. From this perspective you're able to think highly of others. Essentially, humility is a condition of the heart; false humility is pride.

### Encouragement

Encouragement is so important to unity. It is what pushes people on; it is being some else's biggest fan. We must push people to be the best they're called to be. We must believe in them even when they don't believe in themselves. We must encourage them to step beyond what they think is possible, beyond what they think they can do, beyond anything they have ever done. All the while, we become the biggest cheerleader saying, "I know you can, and I know it's possible because of the God who dwells within."

When you're in an organization that encourages you like that, it causes you to soar. Such an organization is incredibly powerful, perhaps even unstoppable. So step up and learn how to create one.

### *Honor*

It's impossible to have unity without honor. Earlier I mentioned the military. In our branches of the military, there is respect for the chain of command and honor for every single one of those positions. They are taught honor in boot camp. But it is evident to me that people in the Church don't know how to honor because it rarely happens.

Unfortunately, some myths have been taught about honor, which is really sad. So I want to show you what honor looks like in the Bible. God thinks honor is pretty important. In fact, honor is mentioned 147 times in the Bible. Let's look at some examples.

Barak asked a woman to go with him into battle. Because he was chicken for the moment, he came under the spirit of stupid. He forgot who his God was for a moment. So Deborah said, *"Very well. I will go with you. But because of the way you are going about this, the honor will not be yours, for the Lord will hand Sisera over to a woman"* (Judg. 4:9). She told him that he would not get the honor because he had not stepped up to his rightful position. The honor will be hers because she would defeat their enemy. There's Deborah in her stilettos, walking through dirt, all dolled up and her hair teased and combed back, with her highlights, going, "Step up, buddy, or the honor is mine." That one story, for some reason, isn't talked about very much.

We've been told in the church that people, especially leaders, are not supposed to be honored. Please do a search and read the 147 texts that talk about honor. When people tell you that we're not supposed to honor each other, it contradicts about 200 other scriptures. It's a lie. People who say that are afraid of people walking in pride. But they're walking in pride because they're walking in false humility.

Deuteronomy 26:19 will shock your socks off. *"He has declared that He will set you in praise, fame, and honor high above all the nations He has made and that you will be a people holy to the Lord your God, as He promised."* God is talking about honoring *you!*

In First Samuel 2:30, God says, *"...Those who honor Me, I will honor, but those who despise Me will be disdained."* God is saying, "If you honor Me, I will honor you." Honor's pretty important to Him, and honor is very important to people. We see honor in the Bible in the form of coats, sashes, and crowns. Joseph was given a coat of honor. It's being set apart. We need to understand the chain of command that exists in organizations and properly honor the leaders.

The other manifestation of honor is honoring one another. The Bible says to honor your father and mother (see Exod. 20:12). We're to honor each other. The Bible clearly shows us what that looks like because God honored His people. He put a coat of honor over Joseph (see Gen. 37:3). Others were given a crown or sash of honor. The Bible shows us that certain tunics, food, and gifts were used to honor people.

We live in a nation today that has very little honor. Many of us go to churches that have no honor. Our youth today do not know the meaning of honor. You can't steal from somebody's influence and call it your own. We have a society of people who are pillaging each other of honor. Honor is giving credit where credit is due. Honor is verbalizing how someone is seen through God's eyes. So often we're afraid to praise or edify others. We don't want them to get a "big head," so therefore, we don't honor.

Honoring one another is honoring God. God speaks through others. When you honor those whom He has spoken through, you honor Him. For example, God commands you to honor your father and mother. When you do that, you're honoring God. Do you want to know what it means to honor your mother and father? You bring honor to your father's house by how you conduct yourself in your own house. You bring honor to your mother by how you treat others.

Honor is respect. It is the dignity that you give to other people—you allow them to be who they are and to share their story. Honor is recognizing someone who helped you get someplace that you could not reach on your own.

Honor can be as simple as a card, as simple as recognizing someone's strengths. Honor can also be recognizing someone who's going through a hard time. It's a simple touch on the shoulder saying, "You know what? I know things are kind of difficult for you right now, but I'm praying for you." That's honor. Honor is uplifting; it's edifying; it's encouraging. And it's impossible to have unity without it.

Interrupting people is dishonor. Being argumentative is dishonor. Refusing to give someone support is dishonor. Expecting something for nothing is dishonor. Expecting someone to do what you're not willing to do for them is dishonor. A one-way deal is dishonor. I think the best way to look at it is to look at the military and how they are set up. You wouldn't think about not saluting properly. Whether you agree with the orders or not, you have to honor, and you have to support the head.

### Obedience

The final point is obedience. Again, if you were in the military, you know what obedience is all about. Regardless of whether you agree, you know that you need to obey. There are four types of obedience. Really, there's only one true obedience; the others are attempts at obedience.

The first one is *reluctant obedience*. Reluctant obedience is when you have to be pushed to do something. People like this can't figure out why they can't succeed or why their lives aren't blessed. It's because of the reluctance in them that says, "I don't know. I'm just not sure." That's reluctance. There's no blessing with reluctant obedience. In fact, reluctant obedience is an instant curse. God wants wholehearted obedience.

The second form is *grudging obedience*. Those with this attitude say, "Fine! I'll do it! But I don't wanna, and I don't like it." If you have children, you have probably seen them do something like this. That is rebellion, not obedience, and it comes with a curse. Reluctant obedience and grudging obedience cause stress in your life. They cause destiny to be prolonged. They cause hardship, headaches, and division; that's the fulfillment of the curse.

The third one is *willing obedience*. The only reason I can talk about these four levels of obedience is because I have experienced them firsthand. I was the worst with obedience! *Willing* was like a curse word; I would only obey as a martyr. When my husband would take a stand on something he felt strongly about, I would say, "OK, fine! I'll do it" but inside I was saying, "NOOOOO!" But then the Lord convicted me while I was disciplining my son (who was told to do something and was not willingly obeying) as the words were flying out of my mouth. I quickly ran to my bathroom and cried because I was completely guilty of the same thing! I would obey, but I'd obey unwillingly and with a grudge—that does *not* get a blessing. But a blessing does come with being willing to obey.

The fourth form of obedience is *fully abandoned, fully surrendered obedience*. Even though I began to experience willing obedience, I still had fear and no guarantee. I was obeying based on trust. But I still was afraid to be willingly obedient. I would do it. I would push down the grudge, push away the reluctance, and I was willing to obey. But I was still afraid, still not fully trusting. Eventually, I came to the place of fully abandoned, fully surrendered obedience, even though I had no guarantee of any result. This is what Christ exemplified on the Cross, a fully surrendered obedience for your life and mine (see Heb. 5:8). There is a great blessing attached to obedience because it honors God when we fully surrender with abandonment and absolutely no guarantee.

It's impossible to have unity without fully abandoned, surrendered obedience. The Lord has been telling you what you're supposed to do. He's been loud and clear with confirmation, with great signs and wonders. He wants you to obey.

My daughter, when she was in the fifth grade, kept asking me to homeschool her. I said "I can't do that. I wasn't smart in school. I teach adults how to succeed. I cannot teach reading, writing, and arithmetic," but I kept hearing, "Homeschool Arika," and Arika kept begging me. The cry of her heart was to get out of the school and to be home to learn with me.

I was reading my Bible one day and I read about Noah and about Moses. I had this huge revelation that God spoke details to His people. Look at the details that Noah received from God. If he had missed one little centimeter of a detail, none of us would be alive today. However, he heard the details and he obeyed.

I read about Moses receiving all of the laws and all of the strategic things that they were supposed to do. I jumped out of bed onto the floor. I lay prostrate before the Lord and said, "God, I want to hear You like that. I want to hear those details. I want You to tell me what to eat for lunch! I want to hear every little detail." Then I heard an audible voice say to me, "I do. You just don't listen!" After bawling my eyes out, I got up and went to church, and I heard a voice during worship, "Home school Arika." And I said, "I rebuke you, satan, in the name of Jesus."

God is my witness. I said, "I rebuke you, in Jesus' name," and He said, "This is Jesus, and you will trust Me, and you will homeschool

Arika." How gracious and compassionate He is. For almost a year He had been speaking this to me, and I just didn't listen. I didn't know it was His voice. Actually, I didn't want to hear that answer; I just pretended that I did. So I ignored it. Have you ever done that? It's the same as when a child asks the mother for a piece of candy, and when she says no, the child goes and asks the father, wanting a different answer.

By the way, homeschooling turned out to be an amazing experience and something I will always treasure. Arika's been on several missions trips, has recorded a CD, and has had time to develop her musical talents—all things that wouldn't have happened if she were still in private school. I'm so grateful God "made" me do it.

Do you know that He has been directing you, answering certain things for you, putting you in places, and confirming what He's telling you to do? Have you chosen not to hear? It's impossible to receive a blessing unless you obey—in fully surrendered obedience.

*Through your training, my husband Mark and I both learned that we worshiped an idol called fear...and because of that a famine was produced in our lives. The word of God jumped out of your mouth into our hearts, and God revealed to us why we have not moved forward.*

—LAURA M

CHAPTER 9

# WHAT KIND OF SERVANT ARE YOU?

One week my pastor spoke about the Parable of the Talents. I sank in my chair because I was thinking, "Lord, you've given me much, and what have I done with it?" At that point I had been retired for several years. I thought I would never speak again. I was no longer equipping people to succeed in the marketplace—I was at home being a mom. A great conviction came over me, and I repented. I went home, laid on the floor, and said, "Lord, God forgive me. You've given me much, and I'm doing nothing with it."

I went home and read the passage thoroughly and discovered some outrageous truths. I discovered which of the three servants from the Parable of the Talents I was being. And I want you to do the same in this chapter. I want you to discover not only which of the three servants you are, but also how you can get promoted out of the position that you're in right now. Do you want to be promoted?

## GOD IS YOUR PUBLICIST

The first thing you need to realize is that God is the Promoter. You need to learn how to make yourself so valuable that your company, organization, or whatever you want promotion with, will do anything to keep you. Don't worry that your boss doesn't see what you do. God will remind the right person at the right time at the right place who has put in the work, who is committed, who has a good attitude, and He will make a way where there is no way for you to be the one ushered into promotion. But you have to do your part.

Next, you'll want to understand that the marketplace pays for value, not for your need. The only thing that will determine your value in the marketplace is your skill. Proverbs 22:29 says, *"Do you see a man skilled in his work? He will serve before kings; he will not serve before obscure men."* So don't bring your need to the marketplace—you'll starve—bring your skill! We are a chosen generation for God, and since we are children of the Most High God, He wants us to get the promotion when it's available. But it doesn't come without effort.

Let's say there's an open management position in a company and two people are going for it. One is a Christian and one is not. The Christian is doing what he's been taught to do: pray, ask God to open the door, and then sit and watch a favorite rerun. The non-Christian is increasing his skills by taking a few extra classes and learning from the right people to qualify for the position. So you tell me, who gets the job? The answer is obvious, and the reasons for it in Scripture will be revealed through this chapter.

Most of us are sitting around saying "What's on television?" or "Let's buy a lottery ticket." We have a total poverty mindset, like I talked about in Chapter 2. Faith is action. It is not sitting around saying, "Oh, Lord, pay off our debt!" or "Get us in a different neighborhood!" or "Find me a new job!" God is saying, "Shut up already and go to work!" It says that. Not in those exact words, but it says that in the Bible (see 2 Thess. 3:10).

I believe Christians are supposed to prosper, but I also believe we need to do something to make it happen. Are you sitting around waiting for God to bless you when you need something? How do you think it's supposed to work? Do you think that all of a sudden God will just rip you out of the house you're in and drop another one on top of you? Do you think you're going to win the lottery or get lucky in Vegas?

I know this: *The harder you work as unto Him, the more you get blessed.* That's what I know. Most people don't do that.

I'm not saying don't pray. Please do pray and go to work increasing your skills. Have you ever noticed that most of the wealthiest and most influential people in the world are non-Christians? Have you ever wondered why? God is bound by His Word, and those powerful influential people, some without realizing it, are actually following His laws of promotion.

## GOD IS YOUR PROMOTER

God sees what you do, and He also sees what you don't do. He knows when you're naughty and nice. This is the truth, my friend. He sees if you're doing it with the spirit of excellence. He sees if you're doing it diligently. He sees who you're doing it for. If it's all about you and your recognition, then it's all in vain. Work as unto Him, knowing that He's right there beside you every single day, all the time saying, "Yes! Go! You can do it. Keep going."

I have several points to share with you about promotion based on the Parable of the Talents in Matthew 25:14-26. As we examine the different responses of the three servants, we will see the proper responses that will position us for promotion.

### Own Your Ability

In the Parable of the Talents (see Matt. 25:14-26), everyone has a talent. All three servants got something. It says that he gave to "each according to his ability" (Matt. 25:15). All of them got a gift from God "according to their ability." What does that say to you and me?

Have you ever raised your ability? Can you remember when you started off on your job years and years ago? Remember when your abilities stunk? With time, training, and trial and error, your ability improved, and you then mastered the task. As a result, your confidence also grew. This shows us that we are each in charge of our own ability department.

You may say, "But Dani, I'm lacking in the ability department." What are you going to do about it? Give up? Give in? If you don't have much ability, you need to go get yourself trained and equipped. It doesn't matter if you don't know something. Go learn it. It's as simple as that. You can learn to do anything. Isn't that awesome? We are co-laborers with Christ. That means that He carries His 50 bricks and you carry yours. Together, you carry the entire load.

Not only do we need to acquire new abilities, but we also need to nurture the ones we already have. The more you use your abilities, the better they become. The more you invest into your skills, the sharper they become.

### Rise to the Test

In the Parable of the Talents, after the master handed out the talents to his servants, he left. This is amazing to me. He left, and he came back a long time later. Why did he give them the talents and then leave? He wanted to see what they were going to do with them. He was thinking, "OK. I have three people. I'm putting out this challenge, and I'll see who is going to step up." We've done this in companies for years. I'll put a challenge out there and then see who steps up. That's what he did. He gave out the talents. He wanted to see who was going to step up. He did not hover over the three servants.

This is important for the codependent society that we live in; he left. Many of us are hovering over our children, our employees, spouses, church members, in case they make a mistake. It says he left; he let them step up on their own to do what they were going to do. He gave them the gift; and then he left to see what they would do with it.

### Honor the Opportunity

Let's talk about the first servant who was given five talents. This is the Dani version of the Parable of Talents. It says that he left at once and invested the money, causing it to double. He took the five talents that his master had given him and he said, "OK. I think I better find a business." So he went out, he invested in a business, and he doubled his money. He no longer had five talents, but ten.

That part's pretty straightforward. But here's what the first servant didn't do. He did not say, "That master, he's just always giving me this load of work to do and then he leaves. I don't want my boss to get any more credit for my success. I don't want this company to prosper anymore from my efforts. Forget it. I am not doing anything." I know Christians and non-Christians who do that and still expect to be blessed.

You can't sow that seed and expect a good return. You can't work with this attitude as unto the Lord: "I'm not going to help. They haven't helped me. What have they done for me? There ain't no way I can move up anyway. This whole thing is bottlenecked. All the people are already at the top, and I'm just the bottom feeder."

That is not what that first servant did. He was so grateful for the opportunity to go out there and do something. He was grateful because he was given a chance. You've been given a chance to succeed as well.

### Perform With Excellence

It says that the first servant invested the money immediately. He did it with a spirit of excellence. He did it diligently. He wasn't focused on anything else other than, "I'm going to make my master proud."

### Trust Your Master

Here's another thing the first servant did. He trusted his master's character. He said to himself, "You know what? I'm right here right now. I better make the best of it." Can you say honestly that you have given your career, your marriage, and so forth the spirit of excellence that you know you should? If you haven't, it is at least partially because you have not quite had a revelation of the God you serve.

Perhaps you think you've found this little life all by yourself. Don't forget that all of your blessings come by the hand of God (see James 1:17). God is the source of every good thing, and He is trustworthy. God moves the heavens and the earth to make His will come to pass. He does that in your life as well. Just ask with a heart of trust and you shall receive (see Matt. 21:22).

### Don't Compare

Let's talk about servant number two. He did the same thing as servant number one. He went out immediately, and he doubled his profits. He had two talents. He invested two talents, and boom, he prospered.

Let me tell you what servant number two did not do. He didn't whine about only receiving two talents. He did not say, "You got five, and I only got two. I always get the short end of the stick. I never get to win." He didn't do that. He didn't call his friend Ezekiel and say, "Ezekiel, I was with my master today, and he is such a jerk. He gave Shakeem five talents, and I got cheated again and only got two." He didn't do that.

He wasn't ungrateful, and he did not compare what he got to what somebody else got. He did not say, "Well forget it then. When I get five, then I'll make it double and I'll do a good job." We too often think like that: "When I get to that director position, then I'll give it my best shot." "When I get that management position, boy I'm telling you what. Watch out, because I'm really going to shine then."

You have to shine first before you get the position or the promotion. You have to be trustworthy first with what you have before you can be elevated beyond where you're at. That's the only way that it works. He did not say, "That does it. I'm never going to be good enough anyway, so why even try? Nothing ever works out for me anyway. Everyone always winds up getting promoted ahead of me. This is always where I wind up, second best all the time. So what's the point?"

I know you're probably not like this, but I am sure you know somebody like this. Servant number two knew who the promoter was, so he went out and he gave it his best shot. He worked with excellence and diligence, not looking to the right or to the left. He wasn't looking to see who was watching him or to see what somebody else did or didn't get. With total gratefulness, excellence, and diligence, he went out and took care of what he was given. The master came back and doubled the blessing. That's how you get promoted.

### Don't Bury Your Talents

Let's look at my favorite servant, number three. Number three was given a talent, and he dug a hole and buried it. I have to confess to you—that was me not too long ago. I buried my talents. I said I would never speak again, would never teach others to succeed again. I even sold the clothes that I had designed and that I used to wear on stage. I sold everything and settled into my lot as a Christian woman to serve as a mother and wife. I thought there was nothing else for me.

The role of mother and wife is a powerful role. I'm still doing it. At my house, every day when my kids get out of school, I'm with my kids. I travel once a month. I home school my daughter. I'm a cooking freak. I still do laundry. I still do dishes. You can ask anyone who knows me. I'm still a mom and a wife. That is my powerful role.

The Bible says that servant number three dug a hole and buried the talent, and it says, *"He hid his master's* [the Lord's] *money."* The money in your pocket, in your bank account, isn't yours; it's God's. He has entrusted you with an amount, and He is watching to see whether you are taking care of it and investing it wisely, or blowing it.

It's the Lord's money, the Lord's talent, the Lord's gift. Yet this servant buried the Lord's money. All that you have is His; when you fully come to that revelation, you will treat things much more differently. All that you are is His. He knitted you together in your mother's womb (see Ps. 139:13). He set a plan for you before the beginning of the foundations of the world (see Eph. 1:4).

What are you doing with the talents that He has given you? You were born with gifts; you were born with talents. We were all born with something. It is His. What are you doing with it? Are you using it? Do you know that you have a gift or a talent? Do you need to get better at using it?

The third servant hid his talent because he was afraid (see Matt. 25:25). Perhaps he was afraid of failure or rejection. It doesn't say. The question you must ask is, Why am I not using my talents? Do you think that they're not good enough?

Let's read Matthew 25:24:

*Then the man who had received the one talent came. "Master," he said, "I know that you are a hard man, harvesting where you have not sown and gathering where you have not scattered seed. So I was afraid and went out and hid your talent in the ground. See, here is what belongs to you."*

Don't you think it's a little strange that the other two did not feel the same way about the master? I believe the servant who was given the one talent was absolutely ungrateful for what he was given. He probably looked at the other two and said, "How come I didn't get that?" He probably was one of those that said, "That wicked master that I serve. I work so hard, and yet I never get a piece of the action." Or he could have been afraid of disappointing his master and had a confidence issue. He had excuses that left his talent dormant.

The servant was delusional. Of the three servants, two of the servants worked with gratefulness, excellence, and diligence in order to please their master. But the third servant had a judgment against the master and said, "You're a hard man, and I was afraid. So here, you can have what is yours." Isn't that the wildest thing? Why is it that the third one had a completely different point of view than the other two?

Do you have a prejudgment against God in a very similar way? Do you think that no matter how hard you work, no matter how hard you try, it's not going to work for you anyway? That's what the third servant thought. He believed that his master was a wicked man. He did not know the character of his master. Do you know the character of your master? If you really truly knew the character of your master, you would go at it with everything you have. Fear would not fit into the equation. Fear of failure, fear of rejection, and fear of man, would not fit into the equation if you really knew the character of your master.

The first two knew the character of their master. They knew, "I'm going to make him proud, and he will bless me." The last one did not know the character of his master and, therefore, did a wicked thing.

### Pass the Test

All three servants were being tested for a promotion. Two took a risk and made an increase. The third servant didn't past the test. My heart hurts when I see my brothers and sisters not being all that they can be. My heart hurts when I see people putting hindrances in their life when they serve such a glorious God who wants them to succeed and shine. He wants the world to see. He wants to announce, "Look what I've done with My son. Look what I've done with My daughter. That's My workmanship."

## HAVE YOU REJECTED YOUR GIFT?

You may have a gift to sing, and you're not using it, and you're thinking, "Well, it's not good enough." Step out in faith and believe that it is His spirit on your tongue that makes it good enough, that He can make a way where there is no way.

I rejected my gift. The Church wouldn't let me speak because of the way I look. The head of a women's ministry actually said to me, "You know, Dani, the women have a hard time with your long flowing hair, and you're a little busty." Did I ask for this? When you were doing womb service, did you order the size of your nose? Me neither. I went home after talking to this woman, and I said, "OK, God. Do you want me to change all that I am? Do you want me to cut my hair off and not wear any makeup?"

I started praying about it, and I cried. I said, "Lord, do You want me to do these things?" I said, "Take my boldness away, God." For five years, I asked my God, Creator of the Heavens and the Earth, to take away the gift that He gave me, which is boldness. "Take away my boldness, God." I wanted Him to take it away because it offended Christians.

But He said, "I gave you that boldness, and you will use it for My glory. I gave you that hair, and you will use it for My glory. I gave you that body, and you will use it for My glory." This is what He said. *"Just as Esther was trained up for such a time as her time, I have trained you up for such a time as this. You be who I created you to be, and you will conform to the image of Christ, not to the image of man."* For some reason Romans 8:29 has been twisted to lead us to believe that conforming to another Christian's opinion is OK. But it says to be conformed to the image of Christ—not the image of people who are trying to *be* Christ.

Let's examine several reasons why people sometimes reject the gifts that God has given them.

## DO YOU KNOW YOUR GOD?

The first reason is a poor understanding of the nature of God. We need to get our understanding of the character of our God from the Bible. Too many people have believed some pulpit somewhere that said, "Meekness is poverty." That's a lie, and it doesn't say that anywhere in the Bible. And it teaches us to believe that we are not supposed to succeed.

## IS IT ALL ABOUT YOU?

Another reason that some people reject their gift (through forfeit) is by using it for their own glory and recognition. That was me for a lot of years. I used my gifts for my fame, and it was wrong. I'm telling you, it was empty. The Bible says that when you do things to gain recognition from man, you have already received your reward in full and you will not get a reward from God (see Matt. 6:1).

Do not seek your own glory because it is not as rewarding as you think. I know a whole lot of people who are so empty inside. They have fame and fortune, yet they are totally miserable. Rather we should want to be humble and to set a good example with our riches and fame. Are you using your gifts or your talent for God's glory?

## DO YOU FEAR MAN?

Have you hidden your gift and talent because you fear being rejected? Have you hidden it because of the fear of man? God's going to hunt you down for the rest of your life, calling you to fulfill His purpose for your life. You might as well give in now. I'm serious. The Bible says, *"Many are called, but few are chosen"* (Matt. 22:14). You were chosen to do something great.

## DO YOU BELITTLE THE GIFT?

Some hide their gifts because of doubt. They don't think it's going to work. They fear taking a risk on their talent, or they assume it's not really important. But that is belittling the gift from God. They say, "It's nothing. It's no big deal." Perhaps you create beautiful art, but you say, "Oh, that's nothing. It's no big deal. I can't do anything with it anyway."

Do you have a gift with numbers, but you belittle it or compare it to somebody else's gift? Let me tell you something. Whatever your gift is, He wants you to grow it. He gave you your smarts. If you have a great brain, He gave it to you because He wants you to prosper it. If you have a gift in business, He gave it to you because He wants you to double it. If you have a gift with people, He gave it to you because He wants you to prosper it.

Whatever it is that you have, whatever gift and talent that you have, He gave it to you. Do not belittle that gift because that's what the third servant did. He dug a hole and buried it. If that isn't belittling, I don't know what is. Have you from time to time dug a hole and buried your gift?

## SETTLING ACCOUNTS

The last part of the Parable of the Talents says the master returned and "settled accounts with them" (Matt. 25:19). He came to settle accounts with each one of his servants. Let's read it again.

The master said to the first servant *"Well done, good and faithful servant! You have been faithful with a few things; I will put you in charge of many things. Come and share your master's happiness"* (Matt. 25:21). He said the same thing to the second servant (see Matt. 25:23).

He also let them keep their talents. The master gave them talents and let them invest them. The servants both doubled their talents, and the master gave all of the talents to them. But notice that they brought their profits to the Lord. They didn't just keep them or spend them. They brought them back to the master and said, "Here you go," and the master said, "Keep it. It's all yours." Both servants said that, and both received the same response. This tells me that our God is fair. He gave all of the servants a gift.

Have you believed from time to time that God is not fair? I have felt the same way. When you see a car crash where a mom and a baby die, you're like, "That's not fair." But we don't know all the circumstances that were involved, and we also don't know the outcome of the big picture of things. I know this, my God is fair. He is over-fair. He not only gave them the money to get started, but He also let them keep the bounty from it.

He let both servants keep their doubling. He didn't say, "Well listen, little guy, I don't think you're ready to keep the profits, so why don't you go try again?" No, he said, "Keep it." To both of them he said, "Good job. Well done, good and faithful servant. Come and share in your master's inheritance."

Let's get to my favorite one. To the man who had received one talent, the master replied, *"You wicked, lazy servant"* (Matt. 25:26). This reminds me of the Scripture that says, *"...The wealth of the sinner is stored up for the righteous"* (Prov. 13:22).

The master called him a wicked, lazy servant. When we think of wickedness, we usually think of murder, pornography, or something of the sort. But this verse tells us that laziness is wickedness in God's eyes. Not using your talent is wicked. Not doubling the profits is wicked. If you do not use your talent, if you do not go to work, if you do not prosper with what you've been given, if you do not prosper where you're planted, then you are considered wicked. That's what it says. Wow. Let's keep going.

> His master replied, "You wicked, lazy servant! So you knew that I harvest where I have not sown and gather where I have not scattered seed. Well then, you should have put my money on deposit with the bankers, so that when I returned I would have received it back with interest. Take the talent from him and give it to the one who has ten talents. For everyone who has will be given more, and he will have an abundance. Whoever does not have, even what he has will be taken from him. And throw that worthless servant outside, into darkness, where there will be weeping and gnashing of teeth" (Matthew 25:26-30).

This clearly states that not using your talents, your gifts that God has given you, is wicked.

Do you like being punished by God? Me neither. He says, *"For everyone who has will be given more, and he will have an abundance.*

*Whoever does not have, even what he does have will be taken from him.*" God cherishes hard workers. He blesses those who work diligently with the spirit of excellence. Do you want a promotion? Then you better start investing your talent. Start using your gifts without fear, without hesitation, without confusion, without all this stuff that the third servant had.

God put us on this planet and is testing us with the chance to get promoted. It's there for all of us, and we're going to make a decision. Are you one who has been given five talents? Are you one with two talents? Are you one who's been given one talent? Don't look at God the way that third servant looked at God. Don't think, "I wasn't given enough," because the same process of promotion worked for all three, and it's according to our ability.

I have spent the past 20 years advancing my ability. My husband and I both have invested tens of thousands of dollars in our skill sets. Have you? When you increase your skills and abilities then you show Him that you have doubled what you've been given, then the Bible says that He will give you more and He will allow you to keep what He gave you. This message is for you to say, "God, I agree with you. I'm going to make you proud."

I want you to be like the other two servants, who came to Him and said, "Look what I've done." Say, "God, look what I've done. This is what You've given me, and I'm making the best out of it." Stop comparing your talents to other people. Stop looking at theirs to determine your value. You must be grateful and say, "God, thank you. I'm going to cherish this, and I'm going to invest it, and I'm going to give it my best shot." Will you promise me you'll give it your best shot?

Do you know that God gave you at least two talents? Keep your eyes fixed on Him. Don't ever question why you are where you are. It's the same process of promotion. If you are diligent and you work with the spirit of excellence, He sees what you're doing, and the two are turned into four. Then, if you keep going, the four turns into eight. And the eight turns into 16. Sixteen turns into 32, and 32 becomes 64.

Have you lost your focus by looking at other people's stuff, thinking, "They're better than I am. I'll never get to where they're at." No more. That is a lie from the pit of hell. Don't you dare compare yourself to the one who has the five. You just keep going.

Don't compare. Take care of what He gave you. *"Trust in the Lord with all your heart and lean not on your own understanding; in all your ways acknowledge Him, and He will make your paths straight"* (Prov. 3:5-6). One day, you're going to look up and say, "Wow! I had no idea that I would ever get to this place."

Are you a five talent person? There is a trap set for you called the comfort zone. The trap happens when you compare your results to other people and see that you're so far ahead of others, and you let that be your gauge. Others cannot be your gauge because that gets you into a rut and into a comfort zone. Have you compared your results to other people and thought, "I don't have to work as hard because they're so far behind." Continue to advance your skills and learn from others who are ahead of you. Avoid the comfort zone like the plague.

You have to rise up with the five that He has entrusted you with and give it that spirit of excellence each and every day. Don't look to the right or to the left, but keep your eyes focused on Him, saying, "God, I'm going to get better this time. I'm going to go higher this time with You." Don't fall into the trap of becoming the servant with the one, and burying your gift. No. He's given you a lot. It's time to make your Daddy proud. He trusted you with a lot. Now it's time to show Him that He made a good investment.

What number do you think I was? I was not born with the five. I was born with one, and the one thing I had was a spirit of excellence. I gave it my best on a basketball court, and that's it. I was not born with gifts. I wasn't born with talents. I was born with the desire to give it my best. If this one, who spent most of her life underneath a rock, could rise up, then so can you. The same God that promoted me wants to promote you.

*The power of working with integrity and excellence, this is what I have been looking for! I knew there had to be a better way, where people were honored and not abused. You showed us how. Thank you for following your call.*

—Kai D

CHAPTER 10

# SIX TESTS: ARE YOU READY?

As we've established in previous chapters, God has given you gifts. Each of us has a unique combination and expression of gifts, and none is better than the other. Every single month, by the hundreds, we see people dedicating their lives to doing things the right way. People are standing up for what is right and living it.

In this chapter I want to look at six tests, found in the story of Joseph, that determine whether we're ready for our gifts. Let's look at Genesis 37. This is a story about business, promotion, and tests in the promotion, after the promotion, and through the promotion. This story holds a revelation, the cheat sheet for the test.

Genesis 37:2-11 says,

*Joseph, a young man of seventeen, was tending the flocks with his brothers, the sons of Bilhah and the sons of Zilpah, his father's wives, and he brought their father a bad report about them.*

*Now Israel loved Joseph more than any of his other sons, because he had been born to him in his old age; and he made a richly ornamented robe for him. When his brothers saw that their father loved him more than any of them, they hated him and could not speak a kind word to him.*

*Joseph had a dream, and when he told it to his brothers, they hated him all the more. He said to them, "Listen to this dream I had: We were binding sheaves of grain out in the field when suddenly my sheaf rose and stood up right, while your sheaves gathered around mine and bowed down to it."*

*His brothers said to him, "Do you intend to reign over us? Will you actually rule us?" And they hated him all the more because of his dream and what he had said.*

*Then he had another dream, and he told it to his brothers. "Listen," he said, "I had another dream, and this time the sun and moon and eleven stars were bowing down to me."*

*When he told his father, as well as his brothers, his father rebuked him and said, "What is this dream you had? Will your mother and I and your brothers actually come down and bow down to the ground before you?" His brothers were jealous of him, but his father kept the matter in mind.*

The story continues in Genesis 37:12-14 this way:

*Now his brothers had gone to graze their father's flocks near Shechem, and Israel said to Joseph, "...Go and see if all is well with your brothers with the flocks, and bring word back to me." Then he sent him off from the valley of Hebron.*

## TEST NUMBER ONE

*Will you serve others, even those you disagree with, when your dream of success seems so far away?*

Joseph was the second youngest of a large tribe, and he was favored by his father and got this nice, beautiful coat. His brothers hated him because they knew that they were not going to be the heir of the father's tribe, of all of his wealth and estate. So they were really ticked off at this kid. And the father protected him even more.

Have you been in a situation where someone else was treated better than you? Joseph knew that his brothers hated him, but look what he does. He "casts his pearls before swine" (see Matt. 7:6), as some of us do on a weekly basis. If you're telling some people the vision that God has given you, and the plans and purposes that you know He planted in you, you may be "casting it before swine."

Here's a giant character flaw. Joseph had favor from his father and favor from God. The brothers also had favor; they were all princes of the same tribe. However, the other brothers were looking at what they didn't have, instead of looking at what they did have. They were looking at the one thing that the younger one got, which was this ornamented coat. The other brothers were princes; they were wealthy; they had an inheritance. Yet they were not satisfied with that because of envy.

Then Joseph presented his dream, and his brothers hated him all the more. Why in the world would Joseph present this dream to his brothers? He knew they hated him. I believe it was pride. He did it because of pride, to boost his ego. It's possible that he wanted to gain acceptance from his brothers, and he wanted to prove his position, that he was equal to, if not better than his brothers. That is total immaturity, and many of us do it every day. We do it with our spouses, with our bosses, with friends at church, with coworkers, with people all over the place.

Many people are trying to prove their authority, to prove who they are, but all they're doing is provoking envy and jealousy straight out of their brothers and sisters—which is exactly what Joseph did. He provoked envy straight out of his brothers because of his pride, ego, and insecurity, trying to prove that he was something that he wished, he believed, he was to become.

After telling his dreams, Joseph then went and found his brothers grazing the flocks. They saw him from afar and said, "Here comes that dreamer! Come now, let's kill him..." (Gen. 37:19-20). They plotted to kill their younger brother. But Reuben, the oldest brother, stepped in and said, "Don't shed any blood...." (Gen. 37:22). In an effort to rescue Joseph, Ruben suggested that they throw him into a cistern. Judah, one of his other brothers, then suggested that they sell him to the Ishmaelites, and they all agreed.

So they threw Joseph into a pit and sold him to the Ishmaelites for 20 shekels of silver. They took the ornamented robe, tore it up, and mangled it. They sacrificed a goat and dipped the robe in the blood of that goat. The brothers took the coat back to the father and the father covered himself with ashes and dirt. He was distraught, and he pretty much died inside. He was living out his days, but he was dead inside. His favorite son was gone (see Gen. 37:23-35).

So Joseph, the favored son with the ornamented coat, the chosen heir of that particular kingdom, found himself in Egypt as a slave. The lesson is, ego and pride lead to your downfall. Trying to prove that you are accepted, trying to hide your insecurity, and provoking envy and jealousy in others only leads to the destruction of your dream. Joseph had his visions, and within days, he was thrown in a pit, bound-up as a slave, and sold into Egypt.

Before we move on in this story, I have to ask you something. Can you see how envy and jealousy led to a malicious plot? Can you see how they led to murder? They led to murder with Cain and Abel (see Gen. 4:1-12). They lead to destruction and to more lying, cheating, and stealing. I don't want to go any further until you "clean house." If you are battling with envy and jealousy, if you are envious when you see other people succeed, if you are envious when you see other people favored, you have a jealousy streak in you.

If this describes you, I want you to pray this prayer right now.

> *Heavenly Father, please forgive me for being envious of other people's favor, other people's success. I don't want to be that way; I don't like being that way. So, right now, in the name of Jesus, envy, pride, jealousy, get out. In the mighty name of Jesus, I am done with you. You have no power and authority over me. In Jesus' name, amen.*

When envy tries to rise, or cling to you, you say, "Shut up, and go back to hell where you belong. That is not me; I am not an envious person. I am a new creation."

Envy and jealousy will only lead to the destruction of your vision, your dreams, and your goals. Envy says, "I have to take that person out so that I can have what they have." Envy wants to destroy somebody else so that you can have what they have. If you get what they have, it will not last because of what was sown. Whatever you sow in envy, you will reap in envy.

Let's get back to Joseph:

*Now, Joseph had been taken down to Egypt. Potiphar,
an Egyptian who was one of Pharaoh's officials, the
captain of the guard, bought him from the Ishmaelites,
who had taken him there. The Lord was with Joseph
and he prospered, and he lived in the house of his
Egyptian master. When his master saw that the Lord
was with him and that the Lord gave him success in
everything he did, Joseph found favor in his eyes and
became his attendant. Potiphar put him in charge of
his household, and he entrusted to his care everything
he owned* (Gen. 39:1-4).

The Lord gave Joseph success. And He's the only one who gives
any of us success too. If you are not serving Him, how are you going
to get success? You might be thinking, *People succeed without the Lord
all the time.* You're right; it's because the principles work, but the Bible
says, *"Unless the Lord builds the house, its builders labor in vain..."*
(Ps. 127:1). If you don't want to live in vain, then you better live with
Him.

In Genesis 39 we discover not only that God gave Joseph success,
but also that He gave him success in *everything.* Genesis is in the Old
Testament, which means that this was written in Hebrew. In Hebrew,
the word for *everything* means—"everything."

Joseph obviously honored those around him and worked diligently
with excellence. He also learned from those around him as well. This
is co-laboring with God. This is working as unto Him and following His ways. If Joseph was like the rest of the slaves or employees
or workers, he would have not found favor in anyone's eyes. I have a
question for you. What kind of worker are you?

When your master sees that God is with you and that He has
given you success, then you will find favor in the eyes of your master
(your company president, your boss, whoever).

Let's read it again.

> *When his master saw that the Lord was with him and that the Lord gave him success in everything he did, Joseph found favor in his eyes and became his attendant. Potiphar put him in charge of his household, and he entrusted to his care everything he owned* (Gen. 39:3-4).

He started as a slave and prospered so much that he was promoted to the head of his master's household.

Then one day, Potiphar's wife noticed that Joseph was a nice looking man, and she was taken with him and made a plot to seduce him. When they were alone in the house, she said, "Come to bed with me." But He said, "Sorry. Your husband has entrusted everything into my care except for you, and I will honor my God and not touch you," and he left (see Gen. 39:6-10). This is proof that he honored those around him as well as his God.

Later she tried to entice him again. She made sure that no one else was in the house but them. She said again, "Come to bed with me." He refused, and she screamed, grabbed his cloak, and ripped it off of him. He fled naked through the palace while she screamed again, "Somebody help me." She went on to accuse him of trying to seduce her. So she lied. Evil, wicked, lying, cheating, and stealing woman.

Just as Joseph seemed to be reaching a place of success, Potiphar's wife tried to tempt him. He stood up under the temptation. He was a strong man. Do you think it would have been hard to stand up underneath that? But as a result of his loyalty to God and his master, he was lied about and thrown into prison (see Gen. 39:11-20).

Joseph had a vision of being in charge of his whole family. But he found himself a slave in somebody else's house, and then a good looking rich woman invited him, "Come on, let's go to bed." He stood up under temptation and landed in prison.

In his dream, he was the one being served. People were bowing down to him. But in order for him to be promoted to that place, God needed to train him on a few things first. The first test was that he went from being a favored son to being a slave in a foreign land to a foreign man who did not even serve the same God.

He humbled himself and he served. I know that because it says, *"The Lord gave him success"* (Gen. 39:3). You might interpret that as he's sitting there in his recliner and then, boom it just fell on him. But that is not how it works. If you read the Bible from cover to cover, you will find a formula for success. Joseph did not sit there and say, "Oh, well, you know, who are these people anyway? These are just a bunch of heathens. They don't even serve the Most High God. They're just a bunch of Egyptians, you know, talking to Pharaoh, god on Earth. They are not worthy of the work of my hands. Don't you know who I am? Don't you know I am Joseph?"

No, he learned how to serve someone else who did not even share the same spiritual beliefs. When he was a young man, he said, "Serve me. I'm the best, I'm favored, and I'm the chosen son." He didn't have to go out to the flock. Daddy wanted him right by his side. Well, God said, "We're going to have to change some of that." So Joseph ended up serving. My question to you is, "Will you serve no matter where you're at?"

Joseph went from Potiphar's house straight to prison. Guess what happened while he was in prison? The Bible says again, *"...But while Joseph was there in the prison, the Lord was with him; He showed him kindness and granted him favor in the eyes of the prison warden"* (Gen. 39:20-21). He went from favored to slave to favored prisoner. He became a prisoner serving criminals, serving people, who served false gods. That must have been very humbling and not much fun.

That was Joseph's first test; he learned to serve by becoming a slave, by going from being the protected son to the prisoner. What will your attitude be when your vision seems so far away? Joseph had the vision and then, almost immediately, found himself as far away from it as possible. But God gave him success in slavery and in the prison because he had the attitude of the person who was going to lead. He did not stop serving his God. He did not stop honoring his God. He did not stop working with the spirit of excellence. He did not say, "Well, forget it then, it's not going to work. Why even try?"

He did not walk in laziness. No, he prospered where he was planted. You may have a vision. You may be thinking "I want to be successful. I want to build something dynamic." You have to act now as though you are that successful person already.

Whatever was put into his hands, Joseph worked as though he was leading a people. Whatever success God has given you right now, you need to treat that as though it is what you want already. That is what Joseph did. He had a vision; it was far away and he was a slave. But he still sowed into his gifts, while a slave and a prisoner, as though he was already the leader of a nation.

Sadly, that's where most people fail. They think that once they get there, it's over. It is never "once you get there." It is the preparation "for there." Joseph was being trained, as a slave, to lead a nation. He was being trained, as a slave, as a criminal, as a servant, to eventually lead the most powerful nation at that time.

## TEST NUMBER TWO

*Will you perform at your highest ability, no matter how unimportant and unexciting the task seems?*

Test number two was whether Joseph would step up. And he did.

He gave his absolute best shot at whatever he was doing and wherever he was. The Bible says that we are co-laborers with Christ (see 2 Cor. 6:1). You put your 50 in; He puts His 50 in. We're co-laborers with Christ. He who sows sparingly reaps sparingly (see 2 Cor. 9:6).

So Joseph gave it his best shot. There was no whining, complaining, murmuring, self-pity, pride, ego, or "poor me." There was no blame. There was no shame. He knew who sent him, and he said, "OK, I guess I'm going to serve in a prison."

Have you been in situations where you wind up whining and crying—even blaming God? Are you in a situation right now that you don't like? You may be blaming God for that situation or blaming other people.

Here's what you need to realize: He has you exactly where He wants you, and where He has you is where He wants to teach you something. Test number one, again, is learning how to serve even in the humble beginnings. Test number two is stepping up and giving it your best shot as though you were already living your dream.

In the midst of a test or a disaster or when things are not going your way, you need to see, believe in, and walk toward your dream as though it is already reality. That's what Joseph did. Prosper where you're planted. Treat your life, career, and/or business that you have as though it is the success that you want. Treat your marriage or family as though it is what you want it to be. Will you give it your best shot when your vision seems the furthest away?

I lived in a particular house for five years; it was a condo, about 2,000 square feet. When I bought it, it was my dream. I was 21 when I bought it. In one year, I had gone from homeless to living in this beautiful quarter-of-a-million-dollar condo. After a few years, I got tired of the condo, and I wanted to move out, but the market had slipped so badly that if I sold it, I would have lost a lot of money on it.

So I had to wait for the value to come up. I used to complain and murmur about the house all the time. I didn't keep it up. I didn't decorate it. I didn't do anything with it because I thought, "I don't like this thing. I'm tired of this thing." Then the Lord spoke to my heart through Joseph's story. He spoke to me loud and clear, and said, "If you treat this like the big dream house that you want, then the dream house will come."

How in the world can you be trusted with the bigger, nicer house when you don't take care of the one that you're in? You're thinking, "Oh, once I get that house, man, I'd have it spit-shined. My toaster will be sparkling; there'll be no crumbs anywhere." Have you thought this way? Do you have this mentality of "when I get there?"

No, you have to treat it as though it is already. Do you not like your car, and, therefore, you do not clean it? It's dusty, it's trashed, there's stuff broken; you just don't care about it. He is seeing how you are treating what He has already given you, and it determines whether you are being promoted to the next level.

It is impossible to be promoted if you don't take care of what you've already have. That goes for the house; that goes for the husband. Many wives, many husbands, say, "I wish my wife was like this," or, "I wish my husband was like that." I used to do that with my husband, Hans. "I thought, I wasn't supposed to be married to some broke young kid who doesn't talk to anyone—there's no way. How did I wind up with him? I was supposed to be married to a multimillionaire who didn't need my money."

This is what God said to me, "Really? How would you treat that person?" "I'd pamper him. We would have fun all the time. I'd have some awesome meals ready for him when he got home from work. I would look good all the time." And God said, "No, you wouldn't. You'd treat him the way you're treating Hans right now because you don't know how." This is what the Lord showed me. He gave me a vision of my husband standing before thousands, powerfully talking and teaching and training. He showed me this vision of my husband being everything that I wanted to be married to, and God said, "As soon as you can treat him as though he is that multimillionaire, then he will become it. Quit treating him like the 'warehouse man'" (he was working in a warehouse at the time).

Treat that husband or wife of yours as though he or she is already what you want the person to be. You speak life into the situation. As Joseph had a vision all around him, he was saying, "I don't care. I am going to take what I have, and I'm going to practice right here." He was practicing on the slaves; he was practicing on the other criminals that were in that place.

Let's return to our story. The next thing that happened was that a cupbearer and a baker came to the prison. They had been accused of stealing something from Pharaoh, the king. Joseph had a gift of dream interpretation. The cupbearer and the baker heard that he interpreted dreams and they asked him to interpret their dreams. Through the interpretations, Joseph revealed that the baker was guilty and would have his head cut off and that the cupbearer was innocent and would be restored to his position. And it happened exactly as he said it would. The baker's head was cut off and the cupbearer was restored. Joseph said to the cupbearer, "Please, remember me." But the cupbearer forgot (see Gen. 40).

Two years later, Pharaoh was being tormented, night and day, by dreams. None of the psychics, seers, or magicians could discern the meaning. No one had the ability to interpret the dream because it was from God Almighty. And the cupbearer had forgotten about Joseph until God brought him back to his mind.

When you're out there working, are you thinking, "No one is watching what I'm doing. Why am I going the extra mile because no one's paying attention to it anyway? You know, I never get any recognition for what I'm doing." You are trying to serve the wrong people. You're looking for recognition and promotion from the wrong department, from the wrong name on the outside of the door. You're looking in the wrong places. Joseph said, "Please, remember me," and the cupbearer forgot. There he was, in the presence of Pharaoh, seeing that no one could interpret the dreams, and God reminded him.

The cupbearer went to Pharaoh and said, "I know somebody that knows how to interpret dreams." Pharaoh said, "Bring me this man." Joseph went to serve Pharaoh; he interpreted the dreams exactly. Basically the dream was a financial message that there will be seven years of plenty in preparation for seven years of famine. And because of Joseph's interpretations, Pharaoh promoted him to second in command of the nation (see Gen. 41).

Are you in a season of famine right now? Or are you in a season of plenty. If you are in plenty, it is in preparation for famine. When you are in a famine, you are preparing for plenty. Are you stoked that you're in a famine right now? What you do in the famine determines what the plenty is going to look like. And how you are in plenty also determines the discomfort of your famine.

Egypt became the most powerful nation of its time during the famine. It made money during the famine. The favor that God put on Joseph made that nation prosperous. People from the other nations were starving, and they were coming from afar to buy grain, trade for grain, do whatever they could to get some grain.

When the famine hit, Joseph's family, in a far off land, heard that someone in Egypt had food. So Israel sent his sons with gifts and money, "Please go get some food." They went to Egypt, and they had to buy the grain from Joseph. But they didn't recognize him because he looked like an Egyptian. He was tattooed; he was wearing a wig; he was wearing a dress; he had gold necklaces on. It's true! God took one of His chosen people and put him in the heathen marketplace and had him look just like one of them. He had him speak their language and participate with their customs.

I know what you're thinking, *You mean God tattooed the boy;*

*God pierced his ears, and told him to wear a white dress with a gold flap?* Think about how we look at the youth today, tattooed up, holes in their ears. We say, "That's not godly; they need Jesus." Maybe they have Him, and, maybe they've been strategically placed to lead lost souls right to the Kingdom of Heaven. God did it then; He's doing it now. Get your head out of your religious box. How in the world are you going to help them if you're acting like something they don't want to be?

But back to Joseph. After he interpreted the dreams, Pharaoh said, "You are now in charge. You be the one to figure out how to solve the seven years of famine and the seven years of plenty." So Joseph went from favored son to slave in a pit, to falsely accused to criminal serving the guilty criminals, to second highest in command of an entire nation. Pharaoh put him in charge of everything. Pharaoh put him in charge of his household and his entire nation. He entrusted everything into Joseph's hands.

Every time that Joseph was promoted, the Bible says it was because God gave him success and prospered him. Don't think for a minute that your success comes from you.

We are co-laborers with Him; whatever you put out, He doubles it. If you become good at putting out, then He will triple it. If you get even better at putting out, then He will quadruple it. If you get even better at putting out, you're looking at a hundredfold. Do you want to be promoted? Do you feel like you are in slavery right now? Then prosper where you're planted.

Take care of the peanuts that you have and you'll get more. Do you feel like you're in prison, with a warden over you? Do you feel like you're in a dungeon? Then prosper where you're planted; treat it like a beautiful garden, and you'll be promoted out of it. If you can be trusted with the small things, and if you treat it as though it is your vision, then God will see your diligence, and He will promote you. He's the one who exalts the humble (see Matt. 23:12).

# TEST NUMBER THREE

*Will you use and develop your gifts in the midst
of disaster and discouraging circumstances?*

Test number three was whether Joseph would use his gifts in the midst of disaster and discouragement. Certainly Joseph had every right in the world to be discouraged. But he didn't sit there and cry the blues. He wasn't lying on his back crying because of his misery. Instead, he was saying, "This is what I've been given; well, this is what I'll prosper with."

Will you use your gifts even in a bad situation? Will you use your gifts even when the vision seems like it's extremely far away?

# TEST NUMBER FOUR

*Will you apply yourself immediately, when
the opportunity arises, even if the circumstances do not match your ideal?*

The fourth test was whether he would go to work right away. What if Joseph had not interpreted the dreams of the cupbearer and the baker? Opportunity always presents itself; the question is, "Can you see it?" The definition of *luck* is "being in the right place at the right time and knowing it."

Many people will read this same book that you're reading, and they will see it, will catch it, will move forward and go after it. Will you be one of those people? Success is not on trial. Somebody's going to take action; that somebody can be you. Will you go to work when the opportunity arises, and use what you have?

Are you going to read this book and do what happened when the cupbearer and the baker came to Joseph and gave him the opportunity to utilize his gifts? He was in a miserable situation. But he kept his mind going by connecting with God, by seeking God, and by utilizing his gifts.

During discouragement, too many people say, "Oh, phooey with it. I'm going to quit; it doesn't work anyway." Have you done this? No more; you need to obey. Whenever you're going through a time of discouragement or disappointment, it just means that you are facing a promotion. When you are going through discouragement and disadvantage and disappointment, you are being tested for a promotion.

That's what this story shows. But only 2 percent of the population is saying, "Oh well. These are not the best circumstances; however, I'm gonna give it my best shot anyway!" The other 98 percent of the population is just whining.

Will you come through with flying colors? Do you know how loving our God is? He will let you take the test again. If you fail the test you're in right now, you'll have to take it again and again and again. Are you tired of repeating the same test over and over and over? He will chase you for the rest of your life.

You might as well stop messing around, get serious, get busy, get some skill, and get success already because that's your destiny. Joseph didn't blame; he didn't criticize; he didn't condemn; he didn't do any of that. He just said, "All right, I'm just here—I have to succeed no matter where I go. No matter how bad it looks out there, I'm going to give it my best in here."

## TEST NUMBER FIVE

*Will you see God's hand in your circumstances*
*and forgive those who have wronged you?*

Test number five came after Joseph found success. He was the second most powerful man in that part of the world. He had an

Egyptian wife and two children. The famine had come and their barns were full of grain. People from all over were coming to them, buying grain and making him rich. Everything looked great; then all of a sudden, his brothers showed up to get grain.

Joseph recognized them, but they did not recognize him. He eventually revealed himself to them in humility. Let's read it. It is absolutely profound. Before you start reading, imagine what must have gone through Joseph's brothers' heads when they realized who Joseph was.

They had sold their brother into slavery and lied about it to their father. Now years later, they were begging for grain from a man who looked like an Egyptian. But then, suddenly, he took his wig off and spoke in their native tongue, saying, "I am Joseph." Imagine the guilt they had lived with all those years. Imagine their fear at realizing that the brother they'd sold into slavery now had power over their very lives. Imagine them remembering Joseph's dreams and thinking, "Oh no!"

*Joseph said to his brothers, "I am Joseph. Is my father still living?" And his brothers were not able to answer him, because they were terrified at his presence.*

*Then Joseph said to his brothers, "Come close to me." When they had done so, he said, "I am your brother Joseph, the one you sold into Egypt! And now, do not be distressed and do not be angry with yourselves for selling me here, because it was to save lives that God sent me ahead of you. For two years now there has been famine in the land, and for the next five years there will be no plowing and reaping. But God sent me ahead of you to preserve for you a remnant on earth and to save your lives by a great deliverance.*

*"So then, it was not you who sent me here, but God. He made me father to Pharaoh, lord of his*

*entire household and ruler of all Egypt. Now, hurry back to my father and say to him, this is what your son Joseph says: God has made me lord of all Egypt. Come down to me. Don't delay. You shall live in the region of Goshen, and be near me—you, your children and grandchildren, your flocks and herds, and all you have. I will provide for you there, because five years of famine are still to come. Otherwise you and your household and all who belong to you will become destitute"* (Genesis 45:3-11).

Joseph knew who had sent him. He demonstrated no blame, vengeance, anger, bitterness, resentment, or unforgiveness—none. God had used his brothers to train up the young Joseph to not just be ruler over his own tribe, but over the greatest nation in the world at that time.

The vision you have, that you can see, is much smaller than the reality of what it will be. The Bible says, *"No eye has seen, no ear has heard, no mind has conceived what God has prepared for those who love Him"* (1 Cor. 2:9). Do you know Him? Do you love Him? If you are being tested right now, you have a choice whether you pass or fail. Will you know during those times of trial that He was the one who sent you?

It is possible to prosper during a famine if you're wise during the harvest time. If you're wise in the plenty, you will prosper in the famine. Are you tired of starving in the famine? Here's my question to you: When the time arises, will you forgive those who do not deserve it? Joseph did. His brothers certainly did not deserve his mercy and forgiveness.

## TEST NUMBER SIX

*Will you take credit for your success, or will you rightfully give credit to God?*

Test number six is amazing. In it Joseph displays a level of leadership that goes beyond most of the people I've worked with or observed in my life (with the possible exception of one or two people). Joseph did not take any credit for his success. He said, *"It was not you who sent me here, but God..."* (Gen. 45:8). Earlier in the story, when Joseph first met with Pharaoh, Pharaoh said, *"...I have heard it said of you that when you hear a dream you can interpret it"* (Gen. 41:15). Joseph responded, *"I cannot do it. But God will give Pharaoh the answer he desires"* (Gen. 41:16).

At every opportunity that he had to use his gifts, Joseph professed his frailness and said, "I can't do anything without Him, but He has given me a gift, and I will use it." When you reach the place of promotion, another test waits for you. Will you give God the glory, or will you take it for yourself and show that you are in it for yourself? Will you give credit to the one who has equipped you, who has put you in the right places, who has opened doors, who has given you favor, who has made things happen for you?

## ARE YOU PASSING?

In First Timothy it talks about the criteria for an overseer. It says that to qualify for leadership, a person must watch his family. If his children and his wife honor him and he can run his household, then he is capable of leading other people. If he cannot lead his own family, however, then he certainly cannot lead anybody else (see 1 Tim. 3:4-5).

This is how Joseph qualified for leadership too. If Joseph had not been able to lead a household and to lead in the prison, he would not have been able to lead a nation.

Our God is so awesome! Look at the little bit that Joseph had to do. He was trusted with peanuts, and God brought the big-time harvest. Joseph just had to be faithful with a little bit and learn his lessons in the process, and God promoted him. That's huge!

You too, if you want to pass the tests, must use what you have, with all you have, with excellence. You need to stop trying to gain acceptance from your fellow man. You need to stop trying to make people envious of you—trying to prove that you are worthy of their acceptance. You need to care about His acceptance of you—His alone. He's already accepted you. It doesn't matter what they say or think.

You have to stop trying to prove that you're worthy, that you have something. Get over trying to prove it; you already have it. You have to maintain vision in prison. How will you take care of the gifts (relationships, money, possessions, responsibilities, influence, and so forth) that God's given you? If you can be trusted with the small things, God will multiply them greatly.

What an awesome God! He gives us the "rule book" in advance. Have you failed some of these tests? Have you failed all six of them? I have. Here's the good news; you get to take them again. Ask God now to forgive you for the places where you have failed. Forgive yourself while you are at it. And then get ready for your next promotion in life.

*Dani, this is what I've been missing and looking for! God bless!*

—Michael C

# BECOMING ONE OF GOD'S CHOSEN

God has given us a promise, and He says that we can test Him on it. I have tested it, and it is true. It has to do with wealth and abundance.

I don't know where you are right now in your life. I don't know where you are with God. But if you plan on trying to do it without Him, you're going to have some hardcore challenges. I'm not saying that you won't have any challenges with Him, because you will, but it's so much easier when you have the "big G" God on your side.

Do you often feel overwhelmed by what you feel inside and by what you want to do? God has a word for you concerning that. In Matthew 22:14 it says, *"Many are invited, but few are chosen."* (The New American Standard Bible translates it, *"Many are called, but few are chosen."*)

## CHOOSING THE TEAM

Are you a little bit confused by that Scripture? I was when I first read it. Let me break it down and make it really plain for you. Imagine basketball tryouts. That's the many who are called. There's a calling, an invitation for basketball tryouts, but only few are chosen.

Let's compare two of the boys who show up. One boy is the hotshot from last year and says, "I've got this sucker in the bag. I don't even have to work hard. Look at my competition; shoot, I got it." Boy number two is eager. He has his new shoes, shorts, t-shirt; he's ready to play his heart out. He is double dribbling; he is granny shooting. He's fouling people; he can't get down the court dribbling the ball right. But he's hard working, willing, teachable, and hungry. Who will be chosen? Let's find out.

In First Samuel 16, God told Samuel to go to the house of Jesse to anoint one of Jesse's sons as king. Samuel walks into the house, sees this big, burly, beautiful man and says, "That guy looks kingly, he must be the one. He's the eldest son, he's strong, and he's good looking. But the Lord said to Samuel, *"Do not consider his appearance or his height, for I have rejected him. The Lord does not look at the things man looks at. Man looks at the outward appearance, but the Lord looks at the heart"* (1 Sam. 16:7).

David was chosen in the Bible. What about on the basketball team? Is it the pig-headed, unteachable kid who thinks he has it in the bag? Is it the one who doesn't need any help and says, "Don't tell me what to do." Or is it the kid who has no skill, but a great heart? Yes, the kid with the great heart is chosen. Many are called, but few are chosen. Those who are hungry, who are teachable, who have desire, and who are willing to do what it takes—they are the ones who are chosen.

Many are called, but few are chosen. The 12 disciples were quite a group of people. If I were Jesus, I probably would not have chosen them. Think about it. Some or all of the 11 denied Him, doubted Him, did not believe in Him, were unfaithful to Him, and ran from Him during His hour of greatest suffering on the Cross. He spent three years with them, and they took off when danger came. Is that who you would pick?

It's obvious that God chooses differently than we do. When it came to the disciples, God knew their hearts. We see this throughout the entire Bible. The way it works is that many are called. God holds tryouts. A team is chosen. Then the team enters a season of preparation that will enable them to win.

## PREPARE TO WIN

Are you called to lead? One thing determines whether you are chosen to lead—your heart. One thing determines whether you will lead—the preparation. Let me show you how to prepare to lead.

King David had to prepare before he sat on the throne. David was prepared as a warrior. He was a warrior and a worshiper, and he became a very successful king. It seemed to be a pretty good formula. David knew how to get things done. He was totally abandoned, fully surrendered to the Most High God, and he inquired of the Lord on everything.

David was the apple of God's eye, even though he committed adultery and murder (see 2 Sam. 11-12; Ps. 17:8). God promised to establish His Kingdom through David forever (see 2 Sam. 7:16). Jesus was a descendant of David, and His Kingdom is still on this earth today. I am part of that Kingdom. If you are a follower of Christ, you are also part of that Kingdom. That Kingdom has stood for thousands of years and will continue forever.

Many are called, few are chosen. The preparation for David to be a warrior king began when he was a shepherd boy fighting the bear and the lion (see 1 Sam. 17:34-37). The preparation for David to be king involved serving and submitting to another king (see 1 Sam. 16:14-23). He served and he submitted to somebody else's vision before his vision came to pass. He was anointed king at 16 years of age, but spent years in preparation before he actually became king.

Do you feel overwhelmed by the idea of destiny? That's because you think you are supposed to make it happen. In your current state, you can't make it happen. You are in the shepherd boy stage. Of course that destiny seems huge and mighty. When Samuel anointed David as the next king, David probably felt intimidated and wondered how it could ever happen. He probably thought, *Why me? Why not one of my brothers?* But God had a plan, and He brought David to the throne in His perfect timing and way.

Let's look at the preparation of Jonah. I can personally relate to this one, and once in a while I wind up back in the belly of a stupid fish. God told Jonah to go to Nineveh and give a message. Jonah rebelled, "I'm out of here, I'm going to Tarshish." The Lord had something for Jonah to do. But Jonah ran from what he was supposed to do because he thought it was something different than what it really was (see Jon. 1:1-2). You might be running from what you are called to do. Let me tell you. God will chase you for the rest of your life. He chased Jonah, and Jonah ended up swallowed by a giant fish until he repented and obeyed (see Jonah 2).

We see preparation throughout the Scriptures. Esther was prepared (see Esther 1:9,12). Every one of the biblical heroes was prepared through opposition, conflicts, and trials. Are you going through some conflicts, some trials, some earthquakes, some tribulations, as they call them? Through these, God's leaders were prepared for what was to come.

If you are called to lead people, there are several different areas in which you must first be prepared. Let me help you with a few.

### Learn to Deal With People

If you don't deal with people properly, they will not want to follow you. They will not want to listen to you. They will not want to obey and submit. They will not want to be directed by you. If you don't know how to deal with people, there's nothing you can say that will make them follow you. In fact, the people skills that you have right now may make people run from you.

Many are called to lead, but few will step up, learn, and be equipped in how to deal with people. Very few will make that investment. Very few will submit to God in that way.

In dealing with people, obviously pulling out the best in them is an art. It is not easy. The Scripture says to love one another (see John 13:34). Do you really know what that means? I'm not talking about surface love. I'm not talking about loving the easy ones. I'm talking about loving the ones that drive you crazy!

I know the Bible says to love one another, but that is something that is a challenge for me. I must lean on Philippians 4:13, which says, *"I can do everything through Him* [Christ] *who gives me strength."* I need to lean on this Scripture daily in order to love other people. If you don't know what it means to love one another, remember this Scripture. You need Christ to love people.

We need Christ to help us love others because people can be mean, manipulative, and rude. They gossip and they judge. Do you see how easy it can be for people to hate other people? Without God, it's a lost cause. Love is actually a fruit of God's Spirit (see Gal. 5:22). It can't happen without Him.

Second John 1:6 says, *"And this is love, that we walk in obedience to His commands...."* His command is to walk in love. First Corinthians 13:1-8, defines love:

> *If I speak in the tongues of men and of angels, but have*
> *not love, I am only a resounding gong or a clanging*

*symbol. If I have the gift of prophecy and can fathom all*
*mysteries and all knowledge, and if I have a faith that*
*can move mountains, but have not love, I am nothing.*
*If I give all I possess to the poor and surrender my body*
*to the flames, but have not love, I gain nothing.*

Let me add my own: If I can become a millionaire and lead a large group of people, but have not love, I have nothing.

*Love is patient* [Just think about that for one second],
*love is kind. It does not envy, it does not boast, it*
*is not proud. It is not rude, it is not self-seeking...*
(1 Corinthians 13:4-5).

If you are self-seeking, you will scare people away. As I said, you need to learn to love people because it does not come naturally to any of us.

*...It is not easily angered, it keeps no records of wrongs.*
*Love does not delight in evil but rejoices with the truth.*
*It always protects, always trusts, always hopes, always*
*perseveres. Love never fails...* (1 Corinthians 13:5-8).

Galatians 5:13 says, *"You, my brothers, were called to be free. But do not use your freedom to indulge the sinful nature; rather, serve one another in love."* The first step toward dealing with people correctly and leading them well is learning to love them.

### Learn to Manage Conflicts and Trials

If you plan on leading people, then you must learn how to deal with conflicts and trials. You need to understand their purpose. Most people freak out and fret. But Hebrews 12:10-11 says:

*... God disciplines us for our good, that we may share in His holiness. No discipline seems pleasant at the time, but painful. Later on, however, it produces a harvest of righteousness and peace for those who have been trained by it.*

James 1:2-6 says we should consider it pure joy when we suffer painful trials. It says that the testing of our faith develops perseverance and that perseverance must finish its work so that we may be complete, lacking in nothing.

Be honest. Do you usually freak out when it comes to trials? Do you usually fret, blame someone else, or blame yourself for the trials? Or maybe you curse the devil for it. Sometimes it is the devil, and other times it is God disciplining you. If you are dealing with the consequences of your own sin, then you need to repent and grin and bear it. Don't do what many do and take no responsibility, they blame, or shall I say glorify, the devil. The devil has received credit for things he has not even thought of doing. When we take responsibility and repent, then God is glorified in our humility. How do you know if it is God's discipline? It depends on whether you are dealing with the consequences of your own choices or not, whether you are dealing with the consequences of your own issues. Other trials truly train us up. All trials, no matter from what direction, are to expose what is in us that needs to be strengthened so we can learn and grow from it.

If it is not the devil, then it must be Daddy. In the past, I have been disciplined in two different ways, by my health and by my pocketbook. I had a heart attack at age 24, a nervous breakdown at age 25, and a fatal heart condition at age 30. You might ask, "Did God do that to you?" No, I pretty much did it to myself. It was just the consequences of my poor choices.

Have you ever spanked your children? The Scripture says,

*"Spare the rod, spoil the child"* (see Prov. 23:13). Do I really believe that? Absolutely. I have five children, and I will tell you spanking works, no question. I don't beat them like I was beaten, but I will definitely give a swat where and when it is needed. This is done in love of course. I explain it to them and correct them to bring them to a heart full of repentance. I have a system that I follow. They recognize it when they see that look in my eyes. They know, it's time to obey. It's a healthy, reverent fear. It's not the kind of fear I had of my stepdad. That was a hateful fear. As a mom I don't want them to have that kind of fear.

And that's what your Daddy in Heaven does. In Hebrews 12 it tells us to not be upset about it. *"The Lord disciplines those He loves, and He punishes everyone He accepts as a son"* (Heb. 12:6).

Are you one who can't get away with anything? Me too. It is actually part of my name; the name that has been prophesied over me my entire life means, "God is my judge," which is what Daniel means. That means a short leash. Do you have a short leash? For example, you cannot speed without getting a ticket? That is a major short leash. You cannot lie. You can't fib. You can't tell a white lie. That's a short leash.

Being a godly leader means embracing conflicts and trials as useful discipline from the Father. It means seeing the fruit of that discipline in your life rather than complaining about the hardship.

### Learn to Submit to Others

Submission to leaders in our lives and having accountability from others is crucial for anyone who wants to be a leader. If you cannot submit to man, you will not submit to God. The Bible says that we must submit one to another (see Eph. 5:21); it's that simple. If you're the maverick out there doing your own thing by yourself, you have no one holding you accountable. You don't have anyone you can trust. You're trying to make it out there on your own, and you're in trouble.

You're heading for a fall. I'm not suggesting that you have just anyone hold you accountable; that can be a disaster as well. You need someone who has your best interest in mind.

How you follow will determine how others will follow you. If you are the type who says, "I don't need to follow anybody," it should not surprise you when you have a bunch of people around you who won't follow anybody either. How well you do or don't follow will determine how well others follow you.

### Learn to Bridle Your Tongue

In preparation for leadership you need to learn to bridle your tongue. As you read this book, you are being equipped with a very powerful level of leadership. The most crucial part is becoming an *effective* leader, and you do that by controlling what you say.

Proverbs 18:21 says, *"The tongue has the power of life and death, and those who love it will eat its fruit."* If you speak death over people by making statements such as, "They're a bunch of lazy, unteachable, unwilling people who don't follow directions," you just put poison on your crop. Life and death is in the power of the tongue, and you will eat the fruit of what you say.

You might say, "I just have ten lazy people." If that's how you treat the ten, God's not going to trust you with 20 or 10,000. If you speak death over 100, it disqualifies you from leading 1,000. How you treat those you have right now will determine whether you pass "Go" and collect $200 or whether you go straight to jail and have to try again and again and again and again and again. Where are you?

### Learn to Choose Belief Over Doubt

You have to choose belief over doubt. You have to choose action over procrastination. You cannot try to overcome it. You have to step in and say, "I'm going to do this." When you set your mind to it and your mouth follows, your feet begin to move in the direction they're supposed to go. There is no, "I just can't seem to motivate myself." Get up and move. If you just open your mouth and begin to speak it and then you follow your speech, success comes. You don't need to read a book on procrastination. You don't need to read some book on fear and opposition and how to overcome them. Just start speaking life. Start agreeing with life. Start agreeing with action because your feet follow your mouth.

### Learn to Submit to God

When I first heard *submit*, I heard it in the form of, "Submit to your husband." Submit doesn't mean what you think it means. The word *submit* means to respect and honor. Let me share an example from my marriage.

Hans and I, even during our time of hating each other, had a deep, passionate love for one another. We still do to this day. You can ask our friends or anyone on our staff. We passionately love each other. Sometimes that passion turns into an argument, but it always ends in some fun. That's the important thing. But then I learned that *submit* means to respect and honor, and I wept and said, "Wow, I love him passionately. But I hate being around him. I hate the way he does things. I hate this and that." At the same time, I had this deep, passionate love. I realized, "I do not respect one ounce of this man, nor do I honor any part of who he is."

I treated my clients better than I treated my husband. I respected my clients, and I respected perfect strangers more than I respected my husband. The Bible says, *"Wives submit to your husbands..."* (Eph. 5:22); it took an act of God for me to do that, a huge miracle.

So now that we know what *submit* means, we need to apply it to God. Job 22:21-22 says, *"Submit to God and be at peace with Him; in this way prosperity will come to you. Accept instruction from His mouth and lay up His words in your heart."*

Do you feel a calling to lead? If you do not pray, you are stupid.

He's the one who brings the people. If you are not inquiring of Him, He will not trust you to have a good influence over them. I know I don't want to take a chance. We are so blessed that God has placed hundreds of thousands of clients in our hands. That's a pretty big level of influence.

I had to be trusted first. I failed a few times in the beginning, but then I figured some things out. I realized that I can do nothing apart from Him. So I have submitted to Him, prayerfully seeking Him, prayerfully inquiring of Him. *What do I do next? Where do You want me to go? How do You want this done? Give me a sign, show me confirmation. I'm not doing anything without You. I don't want to be anywhere where You are not.* That's my prayer every time I step up to do a seminar. *God, if you're not there, I'm not showing up on that platform.*

I haven't always lived like that. I used to depend on myself and my talent and my ability to succeed in life. I don't anymore because it leads to destruction. If you're not tapping into the source of your talent, you will run out. Then, there you are, left high and dry, like I was—unable to function, unable to talk, not wanting to use any part of my gifts.

God is the one who plants the desire, and He's the one who also takes it away. You may be thinking, *How does this person who speaks life and encouragement and who equips people fall into a depression?* I was doing it in my own strength and talent, putting trust in my ability, putting trust in my personal experience to become a millionaire, and it ran dry. Have you ever run dry before? It's not fun, is it? No matter what you try and no matter what you do, you can't seem to pull it together.

That's when you know you're leaning on your own strength and not the strength of the Most High God. If you are leading a people or if you feel called to lead people, and you are not submitting to God and praying daily, you are being stupid. If you want to get to where you want to go, then you need to start submitting and bowing down to your God daily. Apart from Him, you and I can do nothing.

Have you ever been in a situation where somebody has forced you to submit? It's not fun. God doesn't make you submit; He gives you the choice. It may seem like a hard choice, but submission to God holds so many benefits. When I chose to submit to Him, miracles began to occur in my life.

There are a lot of hurting people, and there's a revival taking place in the marketplace. There is a renewal of God's spirit penetrating walls, boundaries, borders, people, and races. He needs an army; He's developing an army who will go out and fight the good fight of faith, who will go out and represent and glorify His name. That doesn't mean that you go out and get your license to be a minister. I have one, and it's just a piece of paper on my wall.

It means that you have the same authority that I have in Christ. It is the same authority and the same power. You have access to all the same Bible, the same principles. It's up to you. Will you submit to Him? Will you fully surrender all and not care about the outcome? Can you do that? Time will tell.

### Learn to Ask for Miracles

Pray for miracles over your people. You have a people just as Moses had a people. You have a people just like David had a people. You have a people just like Abraham and Isaac and Jacob did. Israel had a people. That's what you have. You might have five, but you have a people.

You need to start seeking God wholeheartedly, with full surrender, not conditionally, not halfheartedly, not with a halfway commitment, not only when you need Him. You need to be fully abandoned. Do what it takes to be chosen. When the choosing comes around, make sure you are the one with the right heart and the right work ethic. Be sure you are ready to be chosen.

*I can implement this "stuff" with my family, my
seven kids, and my husband!*

—TAMI G

## CHAPTER 12

# THE SECRET WEAPON

Are you called to be financially blessed? People too often talk about getting wealth without first addressing why they are experiencing poverty. But I want to lead you into prosperity by addressing greed and its counterpart, generosity. Proverbs 15:27 says, *"A greedy man brings trouble to his family...."* This verse tells us the key to breaking poverty—giving breaks poverty.

I am not going to give you all this information about giving and then guilt you into sending me money. I don't need your cash. I am not a broke pastor. I am not a broke missionary. I am a businesswoman, and I didn't make my money from taking offerings. Please don't read this as pride. My boast is in my God, who is faithful to His word and His principles. I have never taken an offering. I have been sent to give to the needy, not to take from them.

That being said, let's talk about giving. It is possible that you may be robbing God weekly, monthly, and yearly by withholding tithes and offerings. At the same time, you expect to be insanely successful in your career, your family, and your ministry. It's not going to happen.

The wealthy know the concept and live by it. It's God's Law, just like the law of gravity. Second Corinthians 9:6 says, *"Whoever sows sparingly will also reap sparingly, and whoever sows generously will also reap generously."* A greedy man brings trouble on his house. He will have poverty at the end. Wouldn't you hate to make a ton of money and then lose it all? That would be lame, wouldn't it?

## THE IMPORTANCE OF GIVING

The reality is that most people don't give anything anywhere. Only two percent of the Church actually tithes. Isn't that sad? That's why they're broke. Luke 6:38 says, *"Give and it will be given to you. A good measure, pressed down, shaken together and running over, will be poured into your lap. With the measure you use it will be measured to you."* You need to underline this in your Bible and post it on your wall.

Since Hans and I have been giving into the Kingdom of Heaven (so that the provision in the name of Jesus might touch the poor and needy, the widows, the children, and the lost), we have gone through seasons of less, but we have never ever had a need for anything. In my retirement, I walked away from three quarters of a million dollars a year income. That had a huge impact on me and my family. But during that time it was pressed down and shaken together. When something gets pressed down, doesn't it have the appearance of being smaller? When your trash bucket is full, you press it down so that it looks like less; then you can put more in.

You may be going through that right now. You may be in the pressed-down stage at the moment (but that's only if you're giving). If you're not giving, you're being disciplined financially. If you are not sowing, you are being disciplined for not sowing. If your finances aren't growing, it's because you're not giving. That's one reason. Another reason is that you aren't working. If you aren't working, the income isn't going to grow. It's that simple. Remember, that's chasing a fantasy.

Another one of my favorite scriptures is Malachi 3:10. It has this promise:

> *"Bring the whole tithe* [10 percent of your income] *into the storehouse, that there may be food in My house. Test Me in this," says the Lord Almighty, "and see if I will not throw open the floodgates of Heaven and pour out so much blessing that you will not have enough room for it."*

He's saying that if you bring Him 10 percent, you can test Him. If you give generously and obey the Word of God, the Lord says, *"Test Me on this. I will press it down, shake it together, and make it running over. Test me on this. If you sow it into good soil, you will reap a good harvest. Test Me on this. I will bless everything you put your hand to if you take care of the poor."*

It's not about a church. It's about giving where there is good fruit. A true storehouse produces fruit, not deadbeats in the pews who are taking up space and leaving the same as they came in. Those who help the poor will be blessed. Those who turn their faces against them will have many curses upon their heads. An organization worth sowing into will be helping the poor. The Bible talks about giving generously to the poor and the needy.

Tithing has to be in the name of Jesus, and wherever that tithe goes, it has to be done in the name of Jesus. Yes, it could be anywhere. You should prepare to succeed because you're always going to get what you are prepared to receive.

## GIVE WITH A GOOD ATTITUDE

It is important not only to give, but to give with the right attitude. Be careful not to harbor wicked thoughts. God loves a cheerful giver (see 2 Cor. 9:7). If you obey willingly, then you get a blessing. If you are being manipulated to give, then the giving is futile. Give in obedience to Him, not because of the manipulation of man.

Don't give with a grudging heart; the Lord will bless everything that you do wholeheartedly. Deuteronomy 15:10 says: *"Give generously to him [the needy] and do so without a grudging heart; then because of this the Lord your God will bless you in all your work and in everything you put your hand to."*

It says that God will bless you in *everything* you put your hand to do. In the Hebrew, that still means *everything*. But if you don't put your hand to do it, it certainly can't be blessed. God has a blessing already waiting for you. If you don't put your hand to it, you will not receive it.

## GIVE TO GOOD SOIL

Matthew 13:4-9 explains reaping and sowing and the different types of soil. We talked about the four types of soil earlier: hard soil (clay), rocky soil, thorny soil, and fertile soil. Only one soil is fertile. Only one soil has a promise, and the promise is 30-, 60-, and 100-fold return. That is fertile ground. If you've been sowing in rocky, thorny, or hard ground, your investment has not reproduced itself. The only way to get the 30-, 60-, and 100-fold blessing on what you have sown is to sow it into fertile ground.

How do you recognize fertile ground? A person or ministry that is fertile ground sees souls being saved. You need to ask yourself, *Where is the money going? What fruit is being produced?* You might attend a dead church that has not grown in 25 years. You're sowing into that ground, and things are not growing back to you because it's clay, and nothing grows in clay. Nothing grows in sand.

Good soil produces good fruit (see Matt. 7:15-20). The places you give should work under the Great Commission, going into all the earth and preaching the Gospel, winning souls, casting out demons, healing the sick, restoring blind eyes and deaf ears, cleansing lepers, and setting captives free (see Matt. 28:19-20).

I am about to tread on some scary ground that will definitely ruffle some serious feathers. But let's look at Matthew 25:31-46 right now. I want you to see who is righteous in the eyes of God. You may be very surprised.

> *When the Son of Man comes in his glory, and all the angels with him, he will sit on his throne in heavenly glory. All the nations will be gathered before him, and he will separate the people one from another as a shepherd separates the sheep from the goats. He will put the sheep on his right and the goats on his left.*
>
> *Then the King will say to those on his right, "Come, you who are blessed by my Father; take your inheritance, the kingdom prepared for you since the creation of the world. For I was hungry and you gave me something to eat. I was thirsty and you gave me something to drink. I was a stranger and you invited me in. I needed clothes and you clothed me, I was sick and you looked after me, I was in prison and you came to visit me."*
>
> *Then the **righteous** will answer him, "Lord, when did we see you hungry and feed you, or thirsty and give you something to drink? When did we see you a stranger and invite you in, or needing clothes and clothe you? When did we see you sick or in prison and go to visit you?"*

*The King will reply, "I tell you the truth, whatever you did for one of the least of these brothers of mine, you did for me." Then he will say to those on his left, "Depart from me, **you who are cursed**, into the eternal fire prepared for the devil and his angels. For I was hungry and you gave me nothing to eat, I was thirsty and you gave me nothing to drink, I was a stranger and you did not invite me in, I needed clothes and you did not clothe me, I was sick and in prison and you did not look after me."*

*They also will answer, "**Lord**, when did we see you hungry or thirsty or a stranger or needing clothes or sick or in prison, and did not help you?"*

*He will reply, "I tell you the truth, whatever you did not do for one of the least of these, you did not do for me." Then they will go away to eternal punishment, but the righteous to eternal life.*

Please compare what man calls righteous and what God calls righteous. There is a major difference. It's not about how often you attend church, or what program you're volunteering for, or what building you're raising money for, or how somebody dresses and speaks or what one does for a living. We've gotten so focused on building buildings and creating programs, instead of caring for the poor. We've become great organizers but poor distributors. We'd rather start a non-profit organization than buy some groceries and deliver them. We've gotten so caught up with the administrative aspect of serving the poor that somehow the simple act of feeding someone has gotten lost. In this passage of Scripture, God is calling the righteous those who care for the needy.

The bottom line is that our salvation is reflected by our giving; that is, where our giving goes, and to whom. This is scary, and unfortunately, there are a lot of places you won't hear this preached because it is a conflict of interest to the building program. The righteous, according to God, are the ones who give to the poor. Notice that both the sheep and the goats called Him "Lord." They were both His followers, so they thought. But what determined the qualifications for those He considered His people was who they gave to. Their giving determined whether they were blessed or cursed.

Those called righteous took care of those on His heart—the hungry, the thirsty, the strangers, the needy, the sick, and the prisoners. Notice that it doesn't say those that built buildings, started nonprofits, or built ministries are righteous. Who was cast into eternal fire because they neglected to care for those in need? The goats; they thought they were His people; in fact, they called Him "Lord." But notice the rude awakening they received.

## IT'S NOT YOURS, ANYWAY

Here's the truth, and I'm going to stand on this truth. You own nothing. God does not need your money. It has nothing to do with you giving money. It has everything to do with the condition of your heart. In the last chapter, we said that *"many are invited, but few are chosen"* (Matt. 22:14). Whether you are chosen has everything to do with your heart attitude.

God owns it all anyway. He just wants to illuminate your heart condition. A stingy man will have his share of poverty. If you are stingy and you don't give, and if you call yourself a child of God and you are not giving ten percent, you're heaping curses on your head. Trust me. I learned this the hard way. I used to think it was all mine, and when it came time to pass the plate, I was not happy with putting thousands of dollars in the bucket. I didn't like it. It wasn't until my heart changed that I was fully, ridiculously blessed, and it has continued to grow. I am floored by how much we have the privilege of giving away in the name of Jesus, not DaniJohnson.com, every single month. It brings me to my knees every time.

You don't own anything. Your kids are on loan. Your car is on loan. Your house is on loan. Your body is on loan. Your spouse is on loan. Your friends are on loan. It's nothing but testing ground and preparation to see what you do with what you have and to determine whether you are ready for the next step.

If your 10-year-old child came to you and said, "Daddy, Mommy, I have a dream. I want to drive a race car 150 miles per hour." Are you going to hand him the keys? No! He is not prepared.

Your Father in Heaven will do the same thing with you. Wealth and success are not in your hands if you are stingy. The quickest way to destroy the curse of poverty is to give and give generously with a cheerful heart. Your Father is not going to put you in your destiny unless you are prepared for it. If you are having a hard time with it, it is between you and your God.

*Thank you for your faith-based program that has not only impacted my business, but my life as well.*

—Becky W

CHAPTER 13

# THE REFINER'S FIRE

I want to give you a secret, a shortcut that I found in Scripture. In fact, it is a humongous shortcut that has made me a tremendous amount of money, saved me money, and saved me from making giant mistakes. It has helped to open doors for us that no man can close and to shut doors that we're not supposed to go through. It has been a secret for protection, a secret for prosperity, a secret for debt reduction, and a secret for absolutely everything. Would you like to know that kind of a secret?

When I was 18, I walked away from God and the Church. I said, "God, if I have to be like your people in the Church, then I want nothing to do with you". I had every reason to feel like I couldn't trust people that were in organized religion. However, eventually I realized that I was judging those people and had to ask forgiveness for the thoughts I had against them. I now love the Church wholeheartedly and have a passion to help people overcome any hurt or rejection they may have experienced. I want to see people succeed instead of being led in different directions.

People in the Church have their problems just like anyone else. None of us are perfect. That's why people like me get hurt. But God has a solution for our issues. He wants His Church to be pure and loving, not a source of pain. He has a process for us, a process of molding and refining. The question is whether we will embrace it or run from it. Do we want to spend our lives fighting and getting nowhere, or surrendering and finding success and fulfillment?

Many people struggle with being afraid of what their future holds. They worry, they wonder, and they just are not sure where they're going. God doesn't want us to be uncertain. If you're uncertain about your future, He wants you to have your eyes opened about where you're supposed to go and what you're supposed to do. You know by now, as you've read through this book, that God wants you to have success. God wants to build His Kingdom, and He's going to use the kings and the priests to do it, which includes you.

But knowing and walking in this vision for your life means that you have to surrender to God's purposes of purification in your life. That is my secret. As I have let go and welcomed His correction and purification in my life, He has rocketed me to a success that I never could have reached on my own. It's a process that we all experience, but if we embrace and welcome it, our benefit will be so much greater.

## PURIFY YOUR LIFE

I want to talk to you about a process of refinement that you are going through, whether you know it or not. It says in Second Timothy 2:20-21:

*In a large house, there are articles not only of gold and silver but also of wood and clay. Some are for noble use and some for ignoble use. If a man cleanses himself from the latter, he will be an instrument for the noble purposes, made holy, useful to the master and prepared to do any good work.*

Would you like to be used for a noble purpose? Whether you are silver, gold, wood, or clay, you can be used for a noble purpose. You can be part of a big, good work. Do you want to be a part of something awesome that makes a difference? Most of us do. You're about to and you don't realize it.

Second Timothy is saying that if we cleanse ourselves, then we will be put to use by the master for a good purpose. Timothy talked about silver and gold. Some of us are silver and some gold. In order for gold and silver to be made precious, they have to be refined. The word *refined* means, "to make fine or pure, free from impurities." Would you like to be free from impurities, free from dross?

According to the dictionary, *dross* is "scum formed on the surface of molten metal, waste matter, worthless stuff, rubbish." When silver is being heated up, the dross is what rises to the top. The dictionary defines *refine* as "purify, clarify, to free from imperfection, coarseness, crudeness; to make more subtle or precious." In other words, the jewelry that you wear on your body has been refined. If it has not been refined, it turns green—or in some cases dark gray, if you're wearing silver. That means it hasn't been refined. All the impurities have not been brought out of it.

Being refined is basically a process that brings forth purity. It gets rid of the junk so that the best, the priceless, the precious stuff can come forward. Most people are afraid of the refining process. They're absolutely afraid to look at themselves. They're afraid to look at what needs to be changed. They'd rather ignore it, and they go through life in absolute bondage, never reaching the freedom and fullness of what they're called to be.

Second Timothy shows us, however, that in order for us to be used nobly, the refinement process has to happen. In order for you to get what you want, the refinement has to happen. So what am I saying? Have you been through hell? Have you been through some hard times? That is the refinement process.

Have you failed over and over again? Have you been tested financially several times by the Lord? This is not an accident. Have you made a lot of money and lost it? This is not an accident. You're going to be refined so that the next time you make money, you keep it. We gain resources during a recession; that's how it works. However, that's only if you have been refined through the last process.

I'm going to talk about clay for a little bit. Isaiah 45:9 says, *"Woe to him who quarrels with his Maker.... Does the clay say to the potter, 'What are you making?'"* Isaiah 64:8 says, *"Yet, O Lord, you are our Father. We are the clay, You are the potter; we are all the work of Your hand."* Jeremiah 18:6 says, *"...Like clay in the hand of the potter, so are You in my hand...."* Second Corinthians 4:7-9 says:

> *But we have this treasure in jars of clay to show that this all-surpassing power is from God and not from us. We are hard pressed on every side, but not crushed; perplexed, but not in despair; persecuted, but not abandoned; struck down, but not destroyed.*

Have you felt perplexed and confused before? Despair comes from the pit of hell, but if you're in the will of God, you are not in despair. Through the molding and refining processes, we don't need to lose hope if we have the end purposes in view.

## SURRENDER TO REFINEMENT

Talking about clay, wood, gold and silver, and the refinement process, we're going to get very uncomfortable. I want you to imagine that you are a lump of clay and that you're in the Master's hand. There you are, and there He is with His wheel. You are His lump of clay, and He is trying to form who you are to be. Perhaps you have been poked a few times, or prodded and stretched. The refining process is very uncomfortable. A pot has to go through the fire in order to become a beautiful piece of art. So the Master sits there and pokes you and presses you and stretches you and slices you and dices you and rips you into two. During this process, many of us are whining and crying and complaining and screaming.

It's the same as kneading bread. Imagine being that poor little lump of dough. You may have gone through this sort of refinement before. But if you haven't, you are about to. Now let me tell you why.

When that pot is formed the way the master wants it, then it goes into the fire for refinement. The fire brings up the bad stuff. So many people do not submit to the fire of God. It's not because the bad stuff is really that great; it's because we have lived in a lie that says, "I don't want to talk about that. I don't want to deal with that stuff. I'd rather live in this lie. It's more comfortable over here." We have wanted a false comfort more than the holiness of God.

So God refines us by putting us through the fire that purifies the bad stuff, then He sits us on the shelf. Have you ever been benched by God? When you're benched, it feels like you're hitting your head up against the wall in your life no matter which way you turn. The pot that needs refining has to sit on a shelf for a certain number of days, and then it is taken off the shelf and put back in the fire again.

Is this your life? You're poked, prodded, ripped in two, sliced, and diced. Then you look beautiful, and you think, *I got it. I made it. I have arrived.* Then He sits you down and says, "Shut up and wait, because I'm not done with you yet." Eventually He brings you back up and heats you up hotter than the first time. But then you're ready to be used.

Are you willing to get the junk out? Are you willing to say, "All right. Send me through the fire. I am done with my dross. I'm done with scum. I'm done with the bad. I'm done with the junk. I can't go on in the way that I'm going on." Are you ready for that?

## FIVE AREAS OF REFINEMENT

There are five areas that have to be refined in you in order for you to succeed wildly in the marketplace, carry the favor of God, be positioned for promotion, be exalted, and so forth. Before you can have any of these things, you have to humble yourself before Him and submit to His refining fire.

### *Unfaithfulness*

Proverbs 13:15 says, *"... The way of the unfaithful is hard."* We all know that hard ways are not pleasant. Proverbs 11:6 says, *"... The unfaithful are trapped by evil desires."* You might be thinking that the word *unfaithful* means "an adulterer." Yes, it does include that meaning, but what I'm talking about here is a little different. I'm talking about being unfaithful to your calling, about having a conditional commitment to your success. *Conditional* means, "If everything goes right, then I will work it out. If I have some people that say yes, then I'll keep going. As long as the company doesn't make any changes, I'll stay." That is conditional living.

Faithfulness is faithfulness, is faithfulness, is faithfulness. Faithfulness means you know who you are serving, why you are here, and what are you doing; it means staying committed to God's vision for your life no matter what. I don't know about you, but I'm here to serve the One who created me. I'm here to do whatever He wants me to do. If He wants to just put me in a brown robe and have me sing in Russian (and trust me, no one wants to hear me sing), then I'll do it. I'm willing to do whatever. If He wants me to be poor or if He wants me to be wealthy, sign me up. I don't care. All I know is that wherever He is, that's where I'll be satisfied.

Conditional commitment, conditional love for your children, conditional love for your spouse, is not what life is about. It is about unconditional attitude. Are you unconditional to people around you? If you're going to be used mightily where you are at, you cannot be unfaithful. You have to be faithful (see 1 Cor. 4:2). If you are faithful to God, He is faithful to you.

For example, if you're not tithing, if you're not giving ten percent straight off the top, you are not being faithful to God (who gave you what you have). That is one area. In the marketplace, if you're going to carry the banner of God, have the favor of God, and see Him make a way where there is no way and open doors that man cannot open, then you better be faithful to Him. You better be faithful to your spouse. You better be faithful to your kids. You better be faithful to serve Him first and Him alone. Do not serve money or greed. There's only one who deserves the highest position—God. If you want to live a life of success, you have to live with faithfulness toward God and those around you.

### Ungratefulness

The definition of the word *ungrateful* is "not thankful for favors." When you look up the word *ungrateful* in a thesaurus it gives you these synonyms: *offensive, atrocious, disgusting, evil, foul, hideous, horrible, horrid, loathsome, nasty, nauseating, obscene, repellant, repugnant, repulsive, revolting, sickening, unwholesome* and *vile*.

Ungratefulness is what kept the children of Israel in the wilderness for 40 years. Ungratefulness leads to murmuring and complaining. When the children of Israel murmured and complained to Almighty

God, they provoked His anger. He wanted to kill them all (see Num. 11:1). He hates ungratefulness.

I want you to look at your life right now. If there is any place in your heart where you are ungrateful, say, "God, help me. Show me. Where am I ungrateful? Where do I have higher expectations on people than I need to? Where do I have higher expectations on myself or on my business that I'm not supposed to have?" Perhaps you believe it's supposed to be a certain way, and when it isn't, you are a little pill to live with. We must not be always looking at the bad, always looking at what's wrong, always looking at what's not working fast enough.

It is impossible for you to be blessed by God when you ungratefully receive a blessing from Him. How likely is He to give you another blessing? How likely is He to give you more favor?

### Covetousness

Romans 13:9 says it best:

> *The commandments, "Do not commit adultery," "Do not murder," "Do not steal," "Do not covet," and whatever other commandment there may be, are summed up in this one rule: "Love your neighbor as yourself."*

In other words, covetousness implies a greed for something that another person has that they rightfully possess. A lot of people covet other people's success. They covet other people's bodies—their figures or the way their bodies look. They covet other people's recognition. They covet people's homes, people's spouses. The grass is always greener on the other side, but it's just as hard to mow. It's the truth. If you can't keep your lawn mowed, what makes you think you could keep that lawn mowed? Coveting is a huge problem in the marketplace, and it's a huge problem for Christians.

It looks something like this: "I want to be where they're at. I want their car. I want their house. How come they always get all the recognition? How can I get that recognition? I want to be looked upon just like them." Lucifer fell from Heaven because He wanted to be just like God; he was coveting God's glory. So his whole plan of attack against every one of us is to get us to want to be like somebody else. That eventually leads us to the very same place that it led him to, the pit of hell.

Covetousness is a state of never being satisfied with what you get, never being satisfied with the results that you work so hard for. I had this all over my life. The first million that I had made was nothing to me. It was like, "Big deal." It wasn't as good as I thought it was going to be. So I quickly became consumed with my next goal—making another million. My motto was, "Gotta go better, faster, harder."

### Idolatry

Colossians 3:5 says, *"Put to death, therefore, whatever belongs to your earthly nature: sexual immorality, impurity, lust, evil desires and greed, which is idolatry."* It says here in the Word that greed is idolatry. The definition of the Greek word for *idolatry* is:

"The worship of idols, images or anything made by hands or which is not God. Excessive attachment or veneration. Veneration, the highest degree of respect; reverence, respect mingled with some degree of awe; a feeling of sentiment, excitement by the dignity and superiority of a person by the sacredness of his character. For anything that which borders on adoration."

Idolatry is the worship of idols, the excessive devotion to or reverence for some person or thing.

I had to be delivered from idolatry because it was prevalent in my life and I didn't even know it. Man is exalted in our culture today, especially professional sports athletes, celebrities, musicians, and movie stars. We have teens with pictures of half-naked women in their room whom they worship because they are thin or beautiful or rich or popular. They literally bow down to them. In my bedroom, growing up, I had a full, floor-to-ceiling picture of Larry Bird. I had an entire wall covered with Larry Bird, and I had everything Boston Celtics. I idolized those basketball players.

Idolatry is huge in America, and it is becoming that way around the world. We idolize movie stars. We idolize speakers. We idolize pastors. We idolize our spouses. We idolize anyone who looks like they are better than us. We hold them up in the highest of esteem. But that position of esteem belongs only to God. He is determined to purify us from our idolatry.

### Greed

The Bible clearly says that idolatry leads to greed (see Eph. 5:5; Col. 3:5). Idolatry of things naturally progresses into wanting more and more of that thing. Greed has a way of lassoing itself around our necks and moving us faster and harder, "I have to have more. I have to have more. I have to get better." "More, more, more! Faster, faster, faster!" Ever deal with that? That was me.

If you're going to be led mightily in the marketplace, if you're going to absolutely wage war out there and take some serious plunder, you better be worshipping the "big-G" God and not the "little-g" god. The "little-g" god is called greed.

If you are obsessing over things—money, fame, your career, any of that stuff—you are on a road to absolute destruction. I know because I've been down the road myself. I lost everything twice because of idolatry and greed. It had me lassoed around the neck and I didn't know it. That is why I've been sent to warn you.

You're being prepared. You have to deal with this stuff. I had to because it is my heart's desire to change and impact the lives of millions of people all over the world, to stand up for what is right, to go after the vision, to encourage them to be all that God has called them to be. However, if I'm easily led by money, it would lead me down a path that wouldn't be toward helping people. It would be toward absolute destruction.

## BE PREPARED TO SUCCEED

Those are five basic areas in which you need purification. If you want to succeed, you absolutely have to be freed from unfaithfulness, ungratefulness, covetousness, idolatry, and greed. The Bible says in Ephesians 5:5-7:

> *For of this you can be sure: No immoral, impure or greedy person—such a man is an idolater—has any inheritance in the Kingdom of Christ and of God. Let no one deceive you with empty words, for because of such things, God's wrath comes on those who are disobedient. Therefore, do not be partners with them.*

God is jealous for your good. He wants you to succeed. He wants you to be blessed and blown away by what He is going to do for you. He loves you so much more than you can imagine. Since He is a loving God, He wants you to be prepared so that you will do and be the best you can be and achieve what your heart desires.

He did it for me—He will do it for you!

*Prior to coming to Dani, I was a recently divorced workaholic who didn't value God, myself, or other people. After plugging into First Steps to Success and Dani Johnson, I paid off over $12,000 in debt in six months. On top of that, I remarried my ex-husband. I'm having more fun than I've ever had in my life, and my confidence is at an all-time high!*

—Kristin H

## CHAPTER 14

# THE WEAPONS OF OUR WARFARE

Fear is a weapon the enemy uses against us, especially with the dart of anxiety. When you battle with worry it is the hand of the enemy shooting fiery darts toward you. However, as the Bible says, our struggle is not against flesh and blood. It's against the principalities of darkness in the spirit realm (see Eph. 6:12). That means that we do not fight worry with flesh and blood.

We fight worry with faith—not faith in ourselves, but faith in Him. He overcame the world. He died on a cross and rose again after three days. He overcame sin and death. He can overcome your mortgage payment. He can overcome your mouthy teenager. I don't care what you're facing. Heart problems are easy for Him. The question is, are you using the weapon of your flesh and blood or are you using His weapons for war?

## FIGHT WITH FAITH

Faith is a weapon. Trust in God is a weapon that can be used against the hand of the enemy. When you trust Him, you'll move out in faith. Obviously, David did not fight with his own strength. He fought with the strength of the Lord (see 1 Sam. 17:45-46). Isaiah 41:10 says, *"Do not fear for I am with you. Do not be dismayed, for I am your God. I will strengthen you and help you. I will uphold you with My righteous right hand."* That's what the Lord says to you. Maybe you're looking at your American Express bill, thinking, "This is so big." But even if it is $50,000, He makes a way where there is no way. How long are you going to let worry, fear, and anxiety be a weapon that can be used against you? The choice is yours.

Matthew 9:18-30 reads:

> *While He was saying this, a ruler came and knelt before Him and said, "My daughter has just died, but come and put your hand on her, and she will live." Jesus got up and went with him, and so did His disciples.*
>
> *Just then a woman who had been subject to bleeding for twelve years came up behind Him and touched the edge of His cloak. She said to herself, "If only I could touch His cloak, then I will be healed."*

*Jesus turned and saw her. "Take heart, daughter."*
*He said, "Your faith has healed you." And the woman*
*was healed from that moment on.*

*When Jesus entered the ruler's house and saw the*
*flute players and the noisy crowd, He said, "Go away.*
*The girl is not dead but asleep." But they laughed at*
*Him. After the crowd had been put outside, He went*
*in and took the girl by the hand, and she got up. News*
*of this spread through all that region.*

*As Jesus went on from there, two blind men*
*followed Him, calling out, "Have mercy on us, son of*
*David!"*

*When He had gone indoors, the blind men came*
*to Him, and He asked them, "Do you believe that I*
*am able to do this?" "Yes, Lord," they replied.*

*Then He touched their eyes, and said, "According*
*to your faith will it be done to you," and their sight*
*was restored.*

Here we see that faith is a total weapon against sickness, death, and disease. Jesus raised people from the dead and said, "Your faith has healed you. Your faith has restored you." The people thought the daughter was dead, but Jesus said, "Oh, no, no, no, no. She is not dead. She is but asleep." Imagine the shame of those who laughed at the Messiah. We must live our lives with faith.

Abraham gives us another example of faith. Romans 8 and Hebrews 11 discuss Abraham. He was 100 years old when he had his promised child, Isaac. It says that Abraham did not even consider his age or the deadness of Sara's womb. Sara was 80! And they had been promised a child. This child would give birth to another child, who would give birth to children, and eventually his descendents would be innumerable. That was the promise that was given to Abraham.

Are you considering your current circumstances to determine your future? If you are, that's a plan of attack from the enemy. The truth is that you have to walk by faith and not by sight. It says that Abraham did not even consider his circumstances. We cannot look at our circumstances to determine our future because our circumstances will make us afraid. Abraham did not do that. He did not even consider.

He was 100 years old and still getting it on with his old wife, expecting a child. Most of us would think, *Yeah right, whatever.* "Come on, honey, we have a promised child to produce." They'd been married for a good 60 or 70 years, and she had never gotten pregnant. But Abraham knew that God had promised, and by faith he believed.

By the way, as a side note, God thinks very highly of sex. Read the Song of Solomon if you want to know what God thinks about sex. I'm telling you, it's steamy. He wants you to have sex with your spouse, and only your spouse. He blesses it.

So, are you considering your circumstances to determine your future? Choose instead to move forward and keep your eyes fixed on Him. God is saying, "I have called you. I know the plan I have for you. It is for good health, for success, for prosperity. God is asking, "Will you agree with Me? Or will you agree with your adversary?" Who are you going to agree with?" That's what it's all about.

Don't you dare consider your circumstances to determine whether you're going to go for it. Don't you dare consider your circumstances to determine whether you're going to make it. Don't you dare consider your circumstances to determine whether you're worthy, whether you're good enough, whether you have enough talent. All of that stuff will burn.

Just consider your God who is faithful, who has called you, not by accident, but by absolute purpose to go into the marketplace and wage war against what the enemy has stolen from you. Go and take back what was promised to you because if you don't take it, others will. They will sow it into pornography, illicit sex, and children's pornography. They will sow it into more debt and more idols. But you will use it for God's Kingdom.

Don't let your impossible circumstances determine what you do. The Israelite army consisted of adult men. In the story of David and Goliath, Goliath said, "I'm going to kill you guys. Come on, give me somebody." And the Bible says that "Saul and his army were terrified." They considered the circumstances. But David did not consider the circumstances. He said, "No way. You know what? You just insulted God. Ooh, you're going to pay for this." (See 1 Samuel 17.)

Attack without hesitation, and fight with the strength and the weapons of the Most High God, not the weapons of flesh and blood. Fight with spiritual forces of faith. Walk by faith and not by sight (see 2 Cor. 5:7). The Bible also says that whatever you ask for and believe you will receive (see Matt. 21:22). In Matthew 7:7 it also says, *"Ask and it will be given unto you; seek and you will find; knock and the door will be opened unto you."*

James says that faith without works is dead (see James 2:14-26). Faith is action. That is why we must ask and seek and knock, which are actions. True faith will be accompanied be actions. There are a whole lot of people asking in their prayer time from their God, "Please get us out of debt. Please Lord, get us out of debt. Oh, Lord, please get us out of debt." They are asking, but not really believing and not acting on that belief. God wants us to ask and have faith and then act on that faith. Faith without action is dead, and the fruit of action is results. Most people talk about faith and have zero results to prove their faith. It's time we all shut up and show our faith by taking action and producing results.

## INTIMATE TRUST

King David trusted God. He had faith. He could trust God because he knew Him. He knew God and that intimacy helped him walk by faith and not by sight. Psalm 92:5 says, *"How great are Your works, O Lord, how profound Your thoughts! The senseless man does not know, fools do not understand."* When we know God, we will know how good and trustworthy He is. Do you know Him? Do you trust Him? Do you say, "God, You brought me here. You gave me a desire to succeed. You designed me to succeed. Oh Lord, I trust You. I believe I am destined for success." Do you then follow up with action? Take the appropriate steps to succeed, don't just talk about it and think about it but produce results.

That is not to say that the road isn't going to be bumpy or that things aren't going to be hard. They will be, I promise you. As we talked about before, the struggles will equip and train you to become better so that you can be given more.

John 15 is one of my favorite passages. In it, Jesus said:

> *I am the vine; you are the branches. If a man remains in Me and I in him, he will bear much fruit; apart from Me you can do nothing. If anyone does not remain in Me, he is like a branch that is thrown away and withers; such branches are picked up, thrown into the fire and burned. If you remain in Me and My words remain in you, ask whatever you wish, and it will be given to you* (John 15:5-7).

You might be afraid to ask. Probably you're afraid He won't give it to you. That's a lie from the pit of hell. Satan wants you to believe that God will not give it to you because if you believe that He will, then you will ask and get it. One of satan's primary weapons is called deception. Whatever he can do to get your attention off of the Most High God, he will do. Whatever he can do to distract your mind to believe in fear and worry and anxiety, he will do. If you focus on those distractions, you will not accomplish what you were set on this earth to accomplish. However, if you believe in what John 15 states, you become a weapon that is used against the kingdom of darkness.

Not only was David not afraid to ask, he also didn't hesitate. Don't hesitate. Have faith. Trust in the Most High God. If you remain in Him, He will remain in you. And the strength of Christ that dwells within you is stronger than he that is in the world (see 1 John 4:4). God, who is stronger than you, is stronger than debt, sickness, death, and disease. He's stronger than your mouthy teens, stronger than your boss, stronger than our government or politics.

My final question to you is this: Do you know Him? Do you know Him like David knew Him? Do you trust Him the way that David trusted Him? Do you have faith like David had? Do you know the Creator of the universe? Do you know the Creator of the Heavens and the Earth? Do you know the "big-G" God, not the "little-g" god? Do you know the Wonderful Counselor, the Almighty God, the one who is slow to anger, rich in mercy, and compassionate? Do you know the Gracious One? Do you know the one who parted the Red Sea? Do you know the Healer, the Provider, the ever-present help in time of need, the Redeemer, the Majestic One, the Holy One, the King who laid His life down for you and me? Do you know The King of kings and the Lord of lords? Do you know the one who strengthens you in your time of need? Do you know your Shield, your Protector, your Comforter, and your Refuge? Do you know Him?

If you don't, you need to.

## THE POWER OF THE TONGUE

The tongue is a powerful weapon that can be used for good or evil, for life or death. Proverbs 18:21 says that life and death are in the power of the tongue and that we will eat the fruit of what we say.

James 3:3-6 compares the tongue to a bit, a small piece of metal, which controls a large horse. Likewise, a ship is a huge vessel controlled by a small rudder. James describes the tongue as an evil fire, as a world of evil among the parts of the body. It corrupts the whole person and sets the whole course of his life on fire. He says, *"...No man can tame the tongue. It is a restless evil, full of deadly poison"* (James 3:8). Fortunately, with God all things are possible (see Matt. 19:26). Apart from Him, we can't bridle our tongue. By His strength, when our tongues are submitted wholeheartedly to Him, they can be bridled.

Many people speak death over their jobs, over their lives, over their businesses, and then they can't figure out why they don't experience growth. Matthew 12:36-37 says, *"But I tell you that men will have to give an account on the day of judgment for every careless word they have spoken. For by your words you will be acquitted, and by your words you will be condemned."*

This is serious. The New King James Version uses the word *idle* instead of *careless.* I looked up *idle* in the dictionary, and *idle* means "inactive." It means "dead, unfruitful, barren, ineffective, and benefiting no one." We will be held accountable on the day of judgment for every ineffective, barren word. *Barren* means "something that doesn't produce fruit." I also gleaned understanding about this from the book *How to Win the Battle of the Tongue* by Dr. Morris Cerullo.

We are always speaking something. The question is, are you speaking life, or are you speaking death? Are you speaking blessing or cursing? Are you speaking worthless, idle, careless words that benefit no one, or are you speaking God's Word that benefits all?

I speak God's Word all day long, sometimes through correction and rebuke, sometimes through lifting people up and calling them to something much higher than where they are. For me, the hard part is speaking God's truth in love and in mercy. I have to literally bridle my tongue with the help of the Holy Spirit because I can't do it on my own.

Morris Cerullo is a minister and speaker who has traveled around the globe and affected millions of people. I highly recommend his book *How to Win the Battle of the Tongue.* It's a great read with lots of truth. One of the things that Morris mentions in his book is that neurologists have proven that the speech center of the brain has total dominion over all the nerves in your body. It has absolute dominion over your life.[1]

I want to tell you something. There is no commitment in trying to make it in your business. There is no commitment in trying to lead well. There is no commitment in trying to become wealthy. There is no commitment in trying. None. Either you will or you won't, and that is determined by your mouth because your actions follow your mouth.

James 3:9-12 says:

> With the tongue we praise our Lord and Father, and with it we curse men, who have been made in God's likeness. Out of the same mouth come praise and cursing. My brothers, this should not be. Can both fresh water and salt water flow from the same spring? My brothers, can a fig tree bear olives, or a grapevine bear figs? Neither can a salt spring produce fresh water.

God is very serious about your tongue. We were created in His image. Through His mouth He spoke us into being. He spoke and the heavens and the earth were created. He spoke and man was created. He spoke and everything above and beneath the earth was created. We are created in His image, but we have not been equipped to use this tongue to create. We've used this tongue to destroy. It has to stop because when much has been given, much is required. Now is the time to bridle this tongue.

### Discerning the Voices

Life and death are in the power of the tongue. Let me tell you the words and the way that the enemy speaks to you so that you can learn what it sounds like.

He speaks through condemnation, confusion, judgment, and criticism. He speaks through fear, guilt, and shame. The enemy speaks through hopelessness, resentment, and blame. He speaks through torment and intimidation.

When you feel intimidated by a person, your adversary is trying to keep you from opening your mouth confidently and speaking life. Intimidation often comes from situations as well—your business, your marriage, your parenting, your ministry. Remember that anything that stops, thwarts, stands in your way, or tears down comes from hell.

The enemy also speaks through depression, oppression, and pride. Let me tell you how pride works (this is why it's important for you to know the Bible). Pride is a nice little whisper that sounds like this: "You are so awesome. You are so good at what you do. Just look at you. You should get more recognition than what you get. You are the one that belongs on that stage. You are so good. There is no one like you. There is no one in this entire company better than you. You're the best." That is pride. Putting yourself down is also pride. Whenever you are the focus, that is pride.

On the flip side, the enemy speaks through false humility. False humility says "I'm really not that good. No, I'm not that good at all. Oh, thank you, thank you. But, really, I gave it my best shot, but I'm really not that good." That is false humility. That is someone who has figured out that saying, "I know I'm awesome," is not good, and they've figured out how to say the same thing with different words.

When someone gives you a word of encouragement and they have spoken life over you, you are to receive it humbly. "Thank you so much for that encouraging word," and let it rest right there. Don't belittle the encouraging word or reject it by saying, "Oh, that was nothing," trying to sound humble. Instead, receive it; it's a word of life that has been spoken over you. Real humility is in the heart and in the heart is where you receive encouragement. Do not let the enemy run away with that encouraging word.

The enemy also says, "Everything is always unfair. Nothing ever works out for you." He speaks through unfairness. He will show you that someone else got promoted and you did not. He will tell you that it should have been your turn instead of their turn. Life is always unfair. The enemy speaks through unfairness.

The enemy also speaks through intellectualism and reason. When God said, "Noah, build Me an ark," the enemy probably said, "What the heck is an ark?" Back then, they did not have bodies of water. They didn't have any boats. But Noah did not sit there and say, "Let me do some research on that." He did not look up *ark*. He did not go to the library and pull up some encyclopedia entries on *ark* on the Internet. He did not go study water. He did not say, "Well, wait a minute, according to my calculations, it has not rained in, let's see, ever. According to my calculations there is no place to put an ark. By the way, how big is it supposed to be?" No, God said, "Noah, build Me an ark," and Noah obeyed. The enemy wants you to reason obedience away, reason action away, and reason faith away.

He speaks through anxiety and stress; he speaks through doubt and "You can't." He speaks through "You're not good enough." He speaks through procrastination. He speaks through apathy and inactivity. He speaks through distractions. He speaks through passivity. He speaks through indifference. "I don't care. What's the use?" He speaks through heaviness, self pity, and retaliation. He speaks in lust. He speaks in greed, and he speaks in hate. Those are just to name a few.

Your Father in Heaven also speaks to you, and obviously you want to recognize and listen to His voice. Let me tell you about the voice of our King, the Most High God. You need to know His voice. Jesus said, *"My sheep listen to My voice; I know them, and they follow Me"* (John 10:27). Your spirit knows His voice, and your spirit desires to hear Him loud and clear. But most of you have spent too much time turning your ears to your adversary and agreeing with what he has spoken to you instead of turning your ears to God and agreeing with Him.

If you've been listening to the wrong side, let me turn on your ears so you can hear God. Your Father in Heaven speaks through grace. He speaks through mercy. He speaks through hope, and He speaks life. Your Father speaks through love and peace. Your Father speaks through faithfulness. He urges you to have self-control. He speaks through joy, abundant joy. He speaks through patience. He speaks through goodness, kindness, and gentleness. He speaks faith. He speaks encouragement.

He speaks "You can do it; I believe in you. Now go!" The enemy likes to use the word *go* as well, but his *go* sounds like, "Go, go, go! Go, go, go, go, go, go!" His *go* is rooted in pressure and intimidation. That is torment. That is not the voice of your God.

The last thing that your Father in Heaven speaks through is a spirit of conviction. Let me tell you what conviction is. The devil cannot create anything, but he is the great counterfeiter. Condemnation is the counterfeit of conviction. Condemnation puts you down. "You stupid idiot, you are lame, and you better not get up again." That's condemnation.

But conviction says, "You made a mistake. You need to make that right." Conviction makes you take a step forward to correct whatever needs to be corrected, and it builds you up in the process. Condemnation tears you down. So your Daddy speaks with conviction, which leads to freedom. Don't ever be afraid of going before the throne of mercy and grace and making a confession, saying, "God, search my heart. Know my ways. There's something in me that needs to change, let's deal with it now." His convicting spirit raises us up; it doesn't put down. Stop submitting to condemnation. Send it back to the enemy the next time it wants to rise up.

Learning to discern the difference between God's voice and the enemy's voice is incredibly important because you will imitate what you are listening to. If you are listening to the enemy's words of death, you will speak death into situations all around you. But if you listen to God's words of life, you will be full of life and will release that life with your words wherever you go.

### Directing Your Tongue

You need to direct your tongue with purpose. David is my greatest hero in the Bible next to Jesus, and in Psalm 17:3 he wrote, *"...I have resolved that my mouth will not sin."* He purposefully directed his tongue (rather than being controlled by it), and with it he powerfully praised God and impacted nations.

If you have had a problem in the past with your tongue, you need to take this warning to heart. I have watched tongues destroy companies, families, 20-year-long relationships, and so forth. There's nothing more destructive than a tongue. It is such a small thing, but such a huge weapon. It's time to use that weapon for you instead of against you. It's time to use it against the enemy instead of for the enemy.

King David's kingdom is still on this planet and has been reigning now for 3,000 years, and it will be a kingdom that reigns for eternity. Would you like to have a kingdom like that? Then purpose your life the way David did. He was a warrior, a worshiper, and a king who said, *"...I have resolved that my mouth will not sin"* (Ps. 17:3). One of the things that he focused on was making sure his tongue agreed with his Father in Heaven instead of with his adversary.

If you read through Psalms, you'll see times where David is saying, "Help me, God. I'm going to die." When you're in the throne room, say anything you like. "God, I'm afraid. I don't know if I can make it, but I put my trust in You and You promised that I would be like a tree that sprouts all year long and that its leaves are always green. You promised. So I put my trust in You."

You need to work on your tongue. You need to speak what is edifying and strengthening. You need to speak what builds up, not what tears down. You need to speak on purpose. Even if it doesn't look right, even if it doesn't sound right, do it anyway. Life and death are in the power of your tongue.

## GUARD YOUR MIND

The mind is a prime place of spiritual warfare. In the New Testament, the Greek word *nike* appears 17 times. *Nike* means "already victorious." It is not something you will be, not something that you might become, not something that is in the future, but *nike* is something that you are right now. It means "already victorious right now."

The bottom line is, "You are already victorious." Remember God planted a desire in you, and it proves the design, which then proves your destiny, which is already within you. This goes back to guarding your tongue and making it agree with the truth. You need to protect the freedom of your mind from the lies that the enemy wants to put into your mouth.

The Bible says, *"It is for freedom that Christ has set us free. Stand firm, then, and do not let yourselves be burdened again by a yoke of slavery"* (Gal. 5:1). Do not return to a yoke of bondage. Resist the enemy and he will flee (see James 4:7). Stand firm in the faith. That's what it says.

First, you need to seek God in prayer, which is another powerful weapon. Seek Him first at all times. He delights in those who diligently seek Him. When you have truly sought Him out, the delight that you will feel is immeasurable. There's nothing to even compare it to, and I mean absolutely nothing.

James says that no man can bridle his tongue unless he submits it to the Holy Spirit. Prayer is an important part of that. Let me teach you how to pray. I don't want to assume that you know how to pray.

If I'm going to equip an army that's going to be deadly against the kingdom of darkness in the marketplace, then you better be a person of prayer.

Here are four steps for how to guard your home, which is your mind, and to stay free from captivity. There are four steps in prayer because what you say with your mouth has a powerful influence over whether you're thinking life or death.

### *Step 1:    Praise*

First I believe you should start with praise, worship, and thanksgiving. All of that is life so it should come first. In Psalm 34:1 David says, *"I will extol the Lord at all times; His praise will always be on my lips."* Praise, worship, and thanksgiving are how you open your time of prayer. I don't care if it's for one minute or five minutes or 20 minutes. In fact I don't care if that's all you do through that entire time. You're breathing life over you. It's out of the overflow of the heart that the mouth speaks (see Luke 6:45), and if you can praise and work in thanksgiving and worship to Almighty God, you will have nothing but life.

Of course that doesn't mean that you won't have disaster fall all around you. But when you have praise on your lips, you know that there is a Savior, a Redeemer, a Reconciler, a Faithful One. Your Comforter, your Strong Tower, is all you know. So you have no worry, fret, or fear, but only, "Lord, I trust You."

Philippians 4:6 says, *"Do not be anxious about anything...."* This is how you will keep your freedom. If you have a tendency to agree with anxiety, stress, frustration, and worry, memorize what I'm about to tell you. *Do not be anxious.* It is not a suggestion; it's a command. Do not be anxious about anything.

Here's the answer. *"Do not be anxious about anything, but in everything, by prayer and petition, with thanksgiving, present your requests to God"* (Phil. 4:6). That is the answer for stress, worry, anxiety, and frustration. Instead of worrying, thank God and tell Him your needs. He is faithful.

### Step 2:  Confession

The second area of prayer is confession. Again, this is just a guideline. Do whatever you want: there's only one thing you must do when you pray (and that's step four). But this is one thing that I choose to do. If I want to lead, if I want a clean heart and clean hands, I better pray in confession. During this time, I confess before my God. "Lord, search my heart. Is there something I need to be forgiven for, or is there someone whom I need to forgive? Is there someone whom I need to bless with my mouth?"

When there's a struggle in my heart over someone who's harmed me, hurt me, spoken something wicked against me, or taken offense to something I have said, I have to lay that at the feet of my Jesus. If it takes root in me, I am in bondage. I hate bondage. The way to destroy it is with confession and forgiveness.

### Step 3:  Petition

The third thing you need to do is petition. Ask Him. Whatever it is, the Bible says all over the place "ask." I did a whole study on the word *ask,* and it's in there so many times that it would take you a long time to read it all. It's not "ask" with an asterisk or a footnote. It's not "ask only if...." It doesn't say anything like that; it just says "ask." John 14:13-14 says, *"I will do whatever you ask in My name so that the Son may bring glory to the Father. You may ask Me for anything in My name, and I will do it."* Anything means anything. *Whatever* means whatever.

Number three is really a promise. Jesus promised in John 14:14 to do whatever you ask of Him so that His Father will be glorified. It's a promise. It's not a suggestion, not a might, but a should. That means that we pray according to His promises, just like my kids petition me according to my promises. "You promised we were going to go to Disneyland. You promised that we would have ice cream after dinner. You promised we were going to have tacos for dinner tonight."

By the way, the Bible says to ask in the name of Jesus (see John 14:14). You have no power or authority unless you use the name of Jesus. If you are not praying in the name of Jesus, what you have spoken was a waste of your time. There's a good chance that some other god (really a demon who is not all knowing or all powerful, but happened to be in the area) caught word of what you asked for. You're letting the wrong side hear your petition.

You must ask in Jesus' name, and you must come boldly before the throne of mercy and grace, knowing that you are a child of the Most High God and that you have His ear (see Heb. 4:16). His arm is not too short; His ear is not deaf. He hears the cries of His people (see Isa. 59:1; Ps. 69:33). Do you believe it? Will you agree with your God who wants to bless you?

### Step 4:  Agreement

Lastly, you need to agree with God and believe His Word. You have to discipline your tongue just like an athlete disciplines his body and diet in order to win. They play to win. They do not go onto the court all frumped out. They do not eat a cheeseburger and super-size fries and milkshake and then get on the basketball court and play the game of their life. Paul actually talks about athletes conditioning their bodies to win in First Corinthians 9:24-27. You must control and condition your tongue to speak life to win.

You need to weigh faith versus feelings or feelings versus fact. We live in a world that caters to people's feelings, and we set up bondage for them. Feelings are nothing more than a road sign pointing to what is in your heart, what has been planted there. You have to size up the feelings to your faith, to the Word of God, to the truth. If your feelings don't match up, you tell them, "Go to hell where you belong."

In spite of your feelings you have to choose to walk by faith and not by sight. It doesn't matter how you feel; life and death are in the power of the tongue. Tell your feelings to shut up. You have to choose to act on faith and not your feelings. The Bible does not say "walk by feelings, not by sight." It says *"walk by **faith**, not by sight"* (see 2 Cor. 5:7).

You have to choose to speak life instead of death. Faith is something that is hoped for, the evidence of things not seen (see Heb. 11:1). The feeling may say in you, "I don't know, maybe I'll be successful." But faith says, "I know, by the grace of God, I will be successful."

Even when you don't feel like it's going to work, you have to walk by faith. Even when you don't feel like it's worth your time, you need to choose to do what you're supposed to do. It is about making a choice. Whenever you say, "I can't," or "I couldn't," you have bowed down to bondage. That's the truth. It is the language of a victim and indicates that someone or something else is in control of you. Regardless of what your feelings are, you have to make a choice. I choose to make it. I choose to believe that His burden is light and His way is easy (see Matt. 11:30).

You have to agree, and you have to choose faith. You have to choose faith over excuses. You have to choose faith over problems, circumstances, and reasons. It's a choice.

As part of agreeing with faith versus feelings, you must refuse to give room or provision to your feelings. Romans 13:14 says that we should make no provision for the flesh or the enemy. *Provision* means "to supply, to make due preparations, to arrange, cater, plan, to fix up with." Not only are we supposed to resist the enemy (see James 4:7), but we also should not give provision to him. This means that when the enemy comes knocking at your door with thoughts of fear, anxiety, doubt, jealousy, coveting, lust, and the like, don't say, "Come on in and have a seat while I entertain you." No way! Do not make room, don't give provision for those thoughts and actions. Shut the door and tell him to go to hell where he belongs.

The Bible says to take every thought captive and make it obedient to Christ (see 2 Cor. 10:5). You have to start thinking about what's in your head. When you finish reading this book, you will have thoughts come at your head. The enemy is going to test your new revelation; he's going to try to plant some seeds of doubt, fear, rejection, and so forth. Your job is to "take every thought captive."

The enemy is the great deceiver. He loves to send confusion, doubt, and hopelessness, which make you think it must be hard, it must be difficult, it must have a very high price for me to get this. That's exactly what the devil wants you to think because those thoughts lead to total destruction. You will not be an effective power in the marketplace against the kingdom of darkness if you allow those kinds of thoughts room in your head. Do not allow the enemy to rob you of your purpose, your inheritance, and your destiny.

## CONCLUSION

Our Father wants us to powerfully impact the marketplace and world, and He's given us powerful spiritual weapons that we can use to fight off the attack of the enemy. He's given you the ammo of faith and trust in God. He's given you the power to speak life with your tongue and to counteract the lies of the enemy by speaking the truth of God. He's also given you the weapon of prayer, which you use to ask for His divine help and to declare His praises. When you speak the truth of who He is, you tear down the enemy's plans.

Now that you know about these weapons, you need to start using them. You are fully loaded; go into battle and take the marketplace as a king. Tame your fears, your uncertainties, your tongue, your thoughts, and emerge as a powerful warrior.

## ENDNOTE

1.    Morris Cerullo, *How to Win the Battle of the Tongue* (San Diego, CA: Morris Cerullo World Evangelism, 1992), 28.

*I have heard the Lord speak to my heart in many ways, and in so many areas, I have been making the wrongs right. My spiritual life with God has changed, and He has been changing me daily. I would rather have Jesus than anything else. I know the rest will come. I could have all the money in the world, but if things weren't right with Jesus, it would all be in vain!*

—CRYSTAL P

## CHAPTER 15

# FACING YOUR GIANTS

When I rededicated my life to the Lord and felt like I could do no good for God because of my profession, the Book of First Samuel had a profound impact on me. I really thought that my profession was my profession and that if I was a really good Christian, then I would become a pastor or some kind of teacher. I had been leading people for 16 years, but I thought I was no good for the Church. I felt for years and years like a lesser person in the Church.

## DAVID'S STORY

But then I read about David in First Samuel. He sliced off heads and foreskins, yet he was the apple of God's eye. Although he was a murderer and adulterer, he was called a man after God's heart. David shatters the religious doctrine that says you better be perfect. God did not set you free for the sake of going into bondage to trying to be perfect. That's not what it's about. They crucified the only perfect One.

As you know, David was 16 years old when he was anointed as king over Israel. Why was David chosen over his brothers? He was the youngest, the baby of the family. He was chosen because of his heart, not because of his skill or ability, not because he was the best or strongest. No, he was chosen because he had a heart after God.

After he was anointed king, David's very first job was to play the harp for the current king. King Saul heard about David's ability to play the harp. God had sent a tormenting spirit to Saul because of his disobedience, and one of Saul's bearers said, "Hey, listen. I know this kid in Bethlehem. He plays the harp, and I hear the spirits leave whenever he plays." Saul said, "I want him."

So David came and began to play the harp for Saul and the evil spirits would leave. David worshiped the Lord in the king's presence, and the demonic spirits left. David's first job as newly anointed king was to serve. That's your first job as a king in the marketplace too—to serve.

We all know the story of David and Goliath. The Israelites were fighting a war against the Philistines. In First Samuel 17:4-7, it says:

> *A champion named Goliath, who was from Gath, came*
> *out of the Philistine camp. He was over nine feet tall.*
> *He had a bronze helmet on his head and wore a coat*
> *of scale armor of bronze weighing 5,000 shekels; on his*

*legs he wore bronze greaves, and a bronze javelin was*
*slung on his back. His spear shaft was like a weaver's*
*rod, and its iron point weighed 600 shekels. His shield*
*bearer went ahead of him.*

Goliath was a giant man who was extremely strong and well-armored. He proceeded to challenge Israel:

*Goliath stood and shouted to the ranks of Israel, "Why*
*do you come out and line up for battle? Am I not a*
*Philistine, and are you not the servants of Saul? Choose*
*a man and have him come down to me. If he is able*
*to fight and kill me, we will become your subjects; but*
*if I overcome him and kill him, you will become our*
*subjects and serve us." Then the Philistine said, "This*
*day, I defy the ranks of Israel! Give me a man and let*
*us fight each other." On hearing the Philistine's words,*
*Saul and all the Israelites were dismayed and terrified*
(1 Samuel 17:8-11).

Goliath continued to issue this challenge every day for 40 days. And the Israelites would run from him in great fear. Then David arrived and heard the challenge. Read what comes next:

*Now the Israelites had been saying, "Do you see how*
*this man keeps coming out? He comes out to defy Israel.*
*The king will give great wealth to the man who kills*
*him. He will also give him his daughter in marriage*
*and exempt his father's family from taxes in Israel."*
*David asked the men standing near him, "What*
*will be done for the man who kills the Philistine*
*and removes this disgrace from Israel? Who is this*

*uncircumcised Philistine that he should defy the armies*
*of the Living God?" They repeated to him what they*
*had been saying and told him, "This is what will be*
*done for the man who kills him"* (1 Samuel 17:25-27).

Next it says that what David had said was reported to Saul, and
Saul sent for him. David said to Saul, *"Let no one lose heart on account*
*of this Philistine. Your servant will go and fight him"* (1 Sam. 17:32).
Saul replied, "Dude, calm down! You're young, man. Cool your jets!"
(That's Dani's version.) David then said to Saul:

> *Your servant has been keeping his father's sheep. When*
> *a lion or a bear came and carried off a sheep from the*
> *flock, I went after it, struck it and rescued the sheep*
> *from its mouth. When it turned on me, I seized it by*
> *its hair, struck it and killed it. Your servant has killed*
> *both the lion and the bear. This uncircumcised Philis-*
> *tine will be like one of them, because he has defied the*
> *armies of the living God. The Lord who delivered me*
> *from the paw of the lion and the paw of the bear will*
> *deliver me from the hand of this Philistine* (1 Samuel
> 17:34-37).

Saul said to David, *"Go, and the Lord be with you"* (1 Sam. 17:37).
Then Saul dressed David in his own tunic and armor. But it did not
fit him, and David said, "I can't move. Can we take this off?" Then
it says:

> *He took his staff in his hand, chose five smooth stones*
> *from the stream, put them in the pouch of his shep-*
> *herd bag and, with his sling in his hand, approached*
> *the Philistine.*

*Meanwhile, the Philistine, with his shield bearer in front of him, kept coming closer to David. He looked David over and saw that he was only a boy, ruddy and handsome, and he despised him. He said to David, "Am I a dog that you come at me with sticks?" And the Philistine cursed David by his gods. "Come here," he said, "and I'll give your flesh to the birds of the air and the beasts of the field."*

*David said to the Philistine, "You come against me with sword and spear and javelin, but I come against you in the name of the Lord Almighty, the God of the armies of Israel, whom you have defied. This day the Lord will hand you over to me, and I'll strike you down and cut off your head. Today I will give the carcasses of the Philistine army to the birds of the air and the beasts of the earth, and the whole world will know that there is a God in Israel"* (1 Samuel 17:40-46).

## CONFRONTING YOUR GIANTS

Are you wondering how this applies to you? Perhaps you are facing some giants right now. Perhaps you're in the middle of a fight. It says that David absolutely went forward after the giant. He did not run; he confronted. Are you running from your giants? Perhaps you have a giant debt or a giant fear. David faced a huge, armored giant; a big, ugly giant with a big mouth. David said to Goliath, "Come on, buddy, let's go at it. Put 'em up; let's go."

Where's your fight? Do your circumstances determine your faith, your strength, and your forward-moving action? If a hundred people tell you no, it should not impact your faith. The bills on your desk, the needs of your house, the circumstances of your life should not determine your faith. If you allow your circumstances to determine your faith, then you allow your circumstances to determine your *strength*. Don't allow your circumstance to determine your fight—you'll lose.

If you want to become a king in the marketplace, as a child of the Most High God, then you must face your giants. That's what David had to do. David is exalted as the most favored king in the entire Bible, next to Jesus Christ. And Jesus Christ even came from the line of David. God honored David so much that He said, "I will establish your house forever," and He has.

In order for you to be a king in the marketplace and used mightily by God, you have to face your giants of fear, debt, opposition, anxiety, worry, and so forth. Slay those suckers. The warrior is what rose up in David. Allow it to rise up in you. The Holy Spirit rose up in David and said, *"Fight the good fight of faith because I'll be with you"* (see 1 Tim. 6:12).

Stop looking at how big your giants are and how small you are, and start looking at how big your God is. Don't focus on how powerful your giants are; focus on the power of the Spirit of the living God who dwells within you. Two thousand years ago He defeated every one of those giants that you are facing today. You have a choice—whose strength will you look at? Only God's strength within you can overcome.

The Bible says that Jesus within me is the hope of glory (see Col. 1:27). It also says that I can do all things through Christ who strengthens me (see Phil. 4:13). It doesn't say "all things except be successful." It doesn't say "all things except get over my debt." It doesn't say "all things except beat my cancer." It doesn't say "all things except honor my boss." It doesn't say "all things except love my spouse." No, it says that *all things* are possible. I don't care how big your giant is; Christ within you can overcome absolutely anything.

The Bible also says, *"...All things are possible to him who believes"* (Mark 9:23). I'm a living testimony to that Scripture. It's Jesus within me who strengthened me to do the things that I did not know I could do. He is a good God. And the devil's a bad devil; he's stupid and he's predictable.

Your God has already defeated the powers of the giant. This is nothing for Him. It doesn't matter what you're facing. No matter how big the problem is, no matter what a disaster it is, God is bigger. These things are nothing but a test of your faith. Will you trust Him? That's the question. Your giant could be disease and sickness in your body, a lack of finances, trouble in your marriage, difficulty with your teenagers, problems at your job, or hurt in your relationships with people.

You have to look back and say, "OK, what did David do?" David killed his giant, and you can too. Let's imitate David's steps to victory.

### Attack Without Hesitation

If the giant is finances, then attack without hesitation. Do what it takes to learn how to get out of debt and increase your skill set so that you can increase your income. Apply yourself with the fervor that David had when he picked up those five stones and said, "Come on, buddy. I do not come at you with javelin or spear or sword; I come at you with the Spirit of the Most High God." That's what David came at him with. He had no fear because his eyes were centered on the One who had delivered him in the past from bears and lions. His eyes were not on his size or Goliath's size, but on the God of Israel who had parted the Red Sea.

He had no fear because fear enters when there is indecision and procrastination. But David did not hesitate. He saw a giant defying the armies of the Most High God, and he said, "Buddy, you're going to die today." And he attacked. So you go and you attack. Attack it big time, knowing that the Bible says, *"If God is for us, who can be against us?"* (Rom. 8:31).

### *Fight With God's Strength*

I love what Ephesians 6:12 says: *"For our struggle is not against flesh and blood, but against the rulers, against the authorities, against the powers of this dark world, and against the spiritual forces of evil in the heavenly realms."* Even though you may be fighting with your spouse, it has nothing to do with your spouse. The Bible says your fight is "against the rulers, against the authorities, against the powers of this dark world and against the spiritual forces of evil." It's the evil forces working within the person that you are fighting, and the battle takes place in the heavenly realms.

We first need to be aware of who we're fighting. We need to see the giant for what it is—spiritual opposition. Then we can take our eyes off of the circumstances and the people involved and get down to battle. In the last chapter, we talked about the weapons of our warfare, but let's briefly review David's primary weapons against Goliaths: faith and trust.

#### Faith

James 2:26 says that faith without works is dead. You have to prove your faith by getting off your butt and getting busy. David could only defeat Goliath by having enough faith in God to get him out on the battlefield. The rest of the Israelites wished God would deliver them, but they had no real faith; otherwise they would have risked their lives, believing that God would back them.

When people are suffering from cancer or some other disease and they are just waiting to die, that is not faith. Faith says: "You know what? I don't care what happens, I am going to go where I have to go; I'm going to do whatever I have to do to have this body be restored. Whatever it is you have for me, I want it; I'll try anything." Faith isn't sitting around waiting for things to happen. The Bible says that when you come to a door you're supposed to knock (see Luke 11:10).

#### Trust

If you want to fight in God's strength, trust is enormously

important. Psalm 28:7 says, *"...My heart trusts in Him, and I am helped...."* David said that. And he lived it too. He trusted God enough to do battle with Goliath. Psalm 84:12 says, *"O Lord Almighty, blessed is the man who trusts in You."* Proverbs 28:25-26 says, *"A greedy man stirs up dissension, but he who trusts in the Lord will prosper. He who trusts in himself is a fool, but he who walks in wisdom is kept safe."*

Let that sink in. "He who trusts in the Lord will prosper," not he who trusts in Dani, not he who trusts in his company, not he who trusts in himself, not he who trusts in the government or the economy, not he who trusts in his house, his spouse, or his boss. No, it says, "...But he who trusts in the Lord, will prosper. He who trusts in himself is a fool, but he who walks in wisdom is kept safe." Wisdom is trust in God. He is worthy of all of your trust.

Ultimately, you must learn to step out like David and defeat the giants in your life. Don't hesitate, and don't try to do it on your own strength. Look to the God who is bigger than any problem, and run forward into battle!

*Before coming to Dani I was a frustrated, burned-out construction company owner who was bored, not enjoying my business and really just going through the motions. With the skill sets I have gained, I have dramatically increased my relationships with my family, clients, suppliers, and employees. My business is exploding in a supposed down market.*

—MARTY R

CHAPTER 16

# SECRETS TO YOUR SUCCESS

"Get an abortion or we're over!" he shouted as he violently slammed the front door of my apartment behind him. The windows rattled in answer to his rage.

I was 17 and had just found out that I was pregnant. It was good news to me, and I remember the scene as if it were yesterday. I had been living on my own, supporting myself with an after-school job, and getting through high school the best way I could. Since Brent and I had been having sex since that summer, I decided birth control was needed. But instead of the pregnancy center giving the pills I needed,

I was given the news of my impending pregnancy. I was shocked, scared, and excited. I certainly wasn't trying to get pregnant, but since it happened, no amount of arm twisting would change my mind.

I stood my ground with all the determination and courage I could muster. There was no way I would give up this baby or kill it. This baby would be the one person I could depend on to love me, and I was excited.

Well, long story short, I was pressured day and night by Brent and his parents to release my baby for adoption to a Christian couple. After weeks of badgering and constant comments like, "What a terrible thing you are doing to this child; it is not fair to the baby. What if your stepfather gets hold of the child and does to the baby what he did to you?" I began having nightmares of the baby being horribly abused like I had been. Terrible, tormenting nightmares continued nonstop, day after day. Even my afternoon naps were disturbed with nightmares. I would wake up gasping for air, crying and screaming at the top of my lungs. The pressure and stress I was under at that time was also a nightmare.

Brent's parents were Christian people in whom I had complete trust and respect. They were people I wished were my parents. I longed to have been raised in a Christian home like theirs and to have parents as loving as they were; parents that didn't fight or do drugs and abuse themselves and their children. *Theirs was the dream home*, I thought. I was vulnerable and naive.

Then they presented a couple to me who promised the moon, the stars, and the earth to get me to give my baby to them. Their "pitch" of an open adoption meant I could see Kristina whenever I wanted, and she could visit me when she was old enough. I could send gifts, receive pictures quarterly, and essentially take an active part in raising her. They were a Christian couple, and they made everything sound so good.

Unfortunately, they delivered on none of their promises, and it was 14 years before I was reunited with my daughter.

# TOO MANY VILLAINS

Throughout my life, I have encountered too many villains to mention in this book. My life has had many tragic let-downs by people who should have upheld integrity and honesty; I was too vulnerable and trusting.

Kristina suffered from these decisions and has abandonment issues, as well as other problems to deal with. In fact, her adoptive parents mistreated and emotionally abused her. They told her they didn't know my name or how to contact me, which was untrue. They even told her I was a prostitute with 11 kids and had given 5 of them up for adoption. Even though they knew I had become successful, they didn't respond to my calls, gifts, letters, and pictures of my other children. Only once every two or three years would I hear from them. It was tormenting.

But then again, trauma was a natural occurrence in my life. In my childhood, it was common to see a lot of blood. I lived a life where people—my mother and sisters—were shoved into sheetrock head first. Walls would crumble and tears would flow. Then there was the sexual abuse by the man in Los Angeles, followed by the physical, mental, emotional, and sexual abuse by my stepfather.

My fairytale marriage turned into *Nightmare on Elm Street*; my great success turned in homelessness; then making millions a second time and receiving accolades and confidence, which turned into business associates and friends embezzling from my business. My bookkeeper, also a trusted friend, embezzled $77,000 from me. The list of trauma includes the story of Kristina and two sets of Christian people.

Any one of these scenarios—the abuse, the manipulation of my baby from my arms, the embezzlements, the deceptive Christians, friends and colleagues, losing all my money, marriage to a con artist—was enough to kill and bury me, or anyone. Certainly it was enough for me to say, "No way will I ever trust anybody ever again," and to look cautiously around every corner. It was enough to make me never want to remarry and to drown myself in drugs, drink, and sorrow. It was enough for me to end it all or commit some kind of a crime and go to prison. This is what happens to some people who have traumatic lives—and I haven't revealed even half of my story nor any gory details.

But I found the key to moving beyond the trauma. Forgiveness.

## *FORGIVENESS* IS THE KEY TO SUCCESS

I can't even tell you where I learned about forgiveness. Back then, I was a metaphysical heathen, and no one ever walked me through forgiveness. Even after going to a Christian school, no one ever told me about forgiving my parents. No one even mentioned forgiveness. No one!

I remember hearing a song on the radio about forgiveness, however. It was "Heart of the Matter" by Don Henley and I used to play it at *First Steps*. Is that where the concept of forgiveness came from? I don't know. But it was definitely the Holy Spirit who brought it into my life. It had to be.

God knows where we are and who is hurting or helpless. His heart breaks for them and for us. He knows. His mercy far extended beyond the drugs I was doing and the sex I was having. His mercy went beyond the crystals I was holding in my hands and the psychics I was talking to. He still spoke to me. I really see the reality of Him leaving the "ninety-and-nine" and going after the one lost sheep.[1]

I knew that I needed to forgive my stepdad—and the others I've mentioned as well as those I haven't mentioned—and I remember honestly how that came about. I knew that when I became homeless, it was evident to me that I had created this disaster in my life. I had held on to so much hatred, anger, and desire for vengeance, rage, deep bitterness, and distrust. The reality of hitting rock bottom like that was too much. Being so afraid to go to a church and anything under the banner of "Christian" was painful. I'd been so deeply, deeply hurt; more deeply hurt by Christians than I ever was by my stepfather. The Christians in my life at that time made my stepfather look like a saint. It was being hurt in a place that was far deeper than being molested, far deeper than being held by my throat and pushed up against the wall. It was far deeper than all the horrible names that I had been called.

## FORGIVENESS DEFINED

Forgiveness is giving up the right to be angry. It's giving up the right for vengeance and malice. It's giving up the right to make the wrong right. It's giving up the right to hatred and retaliation. I don't want to say that it's such a noble thing that I've done. In reality, it's selfish, because I was in bondage to all these things and I needed to be free. On the surface, people look at forgiveness as a noble thing. I'm sorry, but I have to tell the truth. The truth is I needed to be free! I was tired of living with all of the guilt, shame, anger, retaliation, resentment, and distrust. I couldn't live with it any more. I chose the path to freedom. I chose to say, "I hate what you did to me. I hate how you hurt me. But I choose freedom. I choose to forgive. I choose to bless and release you."

God led me to forgiveness with the invitation, "Do you want to be free?" I wanted my freedom. The fruit of forgiveness was compassion overflowing and a freedom that is unexplainable. I realized that if I had been on the same side of the fence, I could have done the same thing. I was just as prone to the same failures as anyone else. I was just as prone as my stepfather and the others who had hurt me. They were taught to behave that way, and it was by the grace of God that

I didn't turn out to be an abuser or molester. It was only by the grace of God, His truth, and His faithfulness.

Forgiveness is big to God, but it is rarely talked about. So rarely do people get walked through the process. People don't confess their sin one to another. They don't confess the things that I am confessing right now. Where is the conviction of forgiveness? It is a hidden thing, unfortunately, because we talk about other things like arguing about the Rapture, and all kinds of doctrinal arguments. None of that leads to freedom without forgiveness. None of that will help me or anyone else to be more like Christ. The key to forgiveness is Jesus dying on the Cross for the forgiveness of our sins.

Look at Joseph. In Genesis 50:17, the Lord asked him to forgive his brothers and the sins they had committed in treating him so badly. I mean, what a shame. Here's this kid thrown into a pit and totally abandoned and abused, but God says to forgive. He did. He forgave his brothers and had a full, clean heart afterward. This is what's so profound and powerful. He knew that it wasn't them. Yes, they committed the act of throwing him in the pit, but it was God who sent him to Egypt. He knew that God was sovereign. He even said to them that it wasn't you who sent me but it was God that I may save the remnant of Israel. That was the plan. It was all used as refinement for him to be groomed and to gain new skill sets.

What did he learn while a slave in Egypt? He learned how to administer an entire nation. Most of us would have stayed in retaliation, bitterness, hatred, and distrust. We would have continued to dwell on all the horrible things people have done to us. But Joseph didn't; he chose to forgive. He knew that it was God, and that God was sovereign. He knew that God brought him there and that He promoted him to the most powerful position in Egypt. Joseph would not have had that kind of success if he was still living in the pit of despair, bitterness, resentment, and unforgiveness.

# TEN POINTS ON FORGIVENESS

## 1.   Forgiveness cleanses.

*If we confess our sins, he is faithful and just and will forgive us our sins and purify us from all unrighteousness. If we claim we have not sinned, we make him out to be a liar and his word has no place in our lives* (1 John 1:9-10). In other words, no confession proves Him to be a liar. Claiming no sin means not confessing. By not confessing, we claim that we have no sin and that what He did at the Cross was useless.

Today, I see Christians everywhere with so much anger and bitterness that they are hurting others because they have been hurt and are not trusting people because they've been around distrustful people. I've watched people do the same thing I once did, trying to hide the pain of their past. We've got to come out with it and be honest about our weaknesses. We spend our entire lives trying to show how strong we are. But in our own strength there is no confession. In our strength there's no weakness to allow God to be strong in our lives.

*Therefore, **confess** your sins to each other, and **pray** for each other so that you may be healed. The prayer of a **righteous** man is powerful and effective* (James 5:16). Again, another misconception of righteousness! So who is He calling righteous? It's those who *confess* to each other and pray for one another.

I believe the enemy works hard on Christians to make sure they don't confess their sins one to another. It's under the deception that "you can't trust them. Your news will be sent all over town." And...and...so? What's that? That's pride. It's self-preservation of your reputation. And what is your reputation? Your reputation is of no avail. God's reputation is the one that's supposed to soar.

Recently, I was talking with a 19-year-old employee of our company. He confessed to being set free from pornography after ten years of addiction. You may wonder how a young kid could be addicted to pornography for ten years? I'll tell you how—the Internet.

Ninety-five percent of all kids have been exposed to pornography. It was not in response to a question I asked, it just poured out of him as an open confession, and I was amazed that he would share this with me.

You know what that confession did for me? "Thank you, Lord, that a kid could be addicted for ten years and You had the power to set him free." It built my faith to know that he was set free from pornography. It didn't make me think any less of him. It made me think more of my God and more of the courage it took for him to confess that he had a problem with pornography. The testimony of Christ prevailed and built my faith.

The devil has us thinking we can't confess our sins. It's a totally different thing to confess our sins to God than it is for us to confess them to each other. It is so much easier to confess them to God. You're alone, it's quiet, you know He will forgive you; you're safe, you might feel some guilt and shame, if you have any remorse at all. But it's an entirely different thing to confess them to others. It's pride that wants to protect our reputations. But it is the Holy Ghost who is being squelched because we won't confess.

I feel so blessed because our clients have learned to walk through forgiveness. They are open books. They are meek and humble with nothing to hide. If they have a drug problem, they confess it.

I have watched the power of confession spur others to get set free, whether from pornography, drugs, greed, pride, debt, alcohol, premarital sex, you name it. I have watched the power of confession bring conviction to another person. Because of confession, the Holy Ghost is allowed to bring conviction to someone else who He wants to see set free as well. I believe this is another reason why the devil works so hard at keeping our mouths shut.

## 2.    *Forgiveness forgets.*

*For I will forgive their wickedness and will remember their sins no more* (Heb. 8:12). He remembers our sins no more and covers all of our unrighteousness. *As far as the east is from the west, so far has he removed our transgressions from us* (Ps. 103:12). This means that we start with a clean slate with Him and that draws us closer to Him. God casts our sins from us never to remember them any more.

### 3.    Forgiveness is a commandment.

*Get rid of all bitterness, rage and anger, brawling and slander, along with every form of malice. Be kind and compassionate to one another, forgiving each other, just as in Christ God forgave you* (Eph. 4:31-32). You cannot get rid of all these negative attitudes and behaviors without forgiveness. Our personal and professional leadership will be hindered when we carry negative attitudes and behaviors. In fact, God cannot and will not expand our territories when we carry bitterness, rage, anger, brawling, slander, and every form of malice. He cannot trust us with other people when we use our influence negatively. But when we fully forgive those who have hurt or hindered us from the past, then the Lord can expand our territories because then our influence is used to honor and build up instead of tear down.

Unforgiveness is a massive hindrance for being promoted in our jobs. It's also a reason why churches and businesses don't grow. It's the reason for divorce and for prodigal sons and daughters. We will not be trusted with influence because we have not done what Scripture commands us to do.

### 4.    Forgiveness ensures your forgiveness.

> *For if you forgive men when they sin against you, your heavenly Father will also forgive you. But if you do not forgive men their sins, your Father will not forgive your sins* (Matthew 6:14-15).

Forgiveness is very important to God. Read the parable in Matthew 18:21-35. It is about a master who forgave his servant an enormous amount of debt. But when the forgiven debtor approached someone who owed him a few dollars, he unmercilessly beat him:

> *Then the master when he heard about what his servant had done, in anger turned him over to the jailers to be tortured until he paid back all that he owed. "I canceled all that debt of yours because you begged me to. Shouldn't you have had mercy on your fellow servant just as I had on you?" This is how my heavenly Father will treat each of you unless you forgive your brother from your heart (Matthew 18: 32-33,35).*

Forgiveness is not a single occurrence. It is not an event or a once in a lifetime thing. It is a daily one, and the only way to keep your heart, hands, and motives clean. It is the only way to draw nearer and nearer to God. Sin separates us from Him, and unforgiveness is an unforgivable sin. Most people think that there is only one unforgivable sin. I say there are two—blaspheming the Holy Spirit is one, but unforgiveness is the other. Unforgiveness is unforgivable because if you will not forgive you brother then God will not forgive you. That's huge!

Peter asked Jesus, *"Lord, how many times shall I forgive my brother when he sins against me? Up to seven times?" Jesus answered, "I tell you, not seven times, but seventy-seven times"* (Matthew 18:22).

> *So watch yourselves. If your brother sins, rebuke him, and if he repents, forgive him. If he sins against you seven times in a day, and seven times comes back to you and says, "I repent," forgive him (Luke 17:3).*

### 5.  *Forgiveness doesn't judge.*

> *Do not judge and you will not be judged. Do not condemn, and you will not be condemned. Forgive, and you will be forgiven* (Luke 6:37).

It's an exchange. If we do not forgive others, we are judging them, and then we will be judged for it. If we don't forgive them, then we are condemning them, and setting ourselves up to be condemned.

Those who are judgmental have very little influence in other people's lives. Those who are judgmental and condemning have a very hard time getting other people to want to follow them or work with them; they can't build healthy relationships. Instead, nasty relationships of distrust and dishonor are built.

### 6.  *Forgiveness and leadership.*

> *So Moses went back to the Lord and said, "Oh, what a great sin these people have committed! They have made themselves gods of gold. But now, please forgive their sin—but if not, then blot me out of the book You have written"* (Exodus 32:31-32).

Moses could have been resentful and unforgiving, bitter and reactive toward the people because when he was delayed in the mountain with God, they quickly made themselves an idol and sinned. He could have said, "You are going to die. God is going to get you! God, get them!" Instead, he was willing to lay down his life for them. But mind you, we hold on to absolute bitterness toward people, and yet Moses had every right in the world to hold on to bitterness toward the stiff-necked, bratty people.

## 7.    *Our prayers and offerings can be hindered because of unforgiveness.*

> *And when you stand praying, if you hold anything against anyone, forgive him, so that your Father in heaven may forgive you your sins* (Mark 11:25).

> *But if you do not forgive men their sins, your Father will not forgive your sins* (Matthew 6:15).

> *Therefore, if you are offering your gift at the altar and there remember that your brother has something against you, leave your gift there in front of the altar. First go and be reconciled to your brother; then come and offer your gift* (Matthew 5:23-24).

Leave your offering at the altar and make peace with your brother. God doesn't even want to touch your offerings until your heart is clean toward your brother. This means that we make offerings all the time with dirty hearts and hands toward loads of people. The offering counts for nothing. So it's clear for us to go make things right with our brother and then return with our offering and He will receive it.

## 8.    *Forgiveness is tied to healing.*

> *Pharaoh quickly summoned Moses and Aaron and said, "I have sinned against the Lord your God and against you. Now forgive my sin once more and pray to the Lord your God to take this deadly plague away from me"* (Exodus 10:16-17).

The plague of locusts swarmed the country of Egypt, except for the area where the Israelites lived, in answer to Pharaoh's hard-heart-edness. After Moses prayed, healing was restored to the Egyptians. God healed the land because the locusts were killing the food supply, which would eventually lead to starvation. That means it hindered their finances as well as their health.

Rebellion spurred on a judgment from the Lord and the judgment that came was attacking the prosperity of the land. Notice Pharaoh said, "...*and pray to the Lord your God to take this deadly plague away from me.*" Why did he want it taken away? The locusts were killing their food and animals, and were destroying their livelihood and prosperity.

Look at this Scripture. *If my people, who are called by my name, will **humble** themselves and pray and seek my face and **turn** from their wicked ways, then will I hear from heaven and will **forgive** their sin and will **heal** their land* (2 Chron. 7:14).

What does it mean to heal the land? The land must have been desolate, full of sickness, death, and disease, and void of prosperity. God said, "I will heal your crops, herds, people, and water. I will heal everything in that land." He promised to prosper that land again if they would humble themselves.

So to me, healing their land means to prosper the land and bring healing to the finances, as well as physical bodies. God's forgiveness will bring healing. It takes seeking Him and *turning* from wickedness for the blessing to come.

### 9.   *Forgiveness produces love.*

> *Therefore, I tell you, her many sins have been for-given—for she loved much. But he who has been for-given little loves little* (Luke 7:47).

Without confession there is no forgiveness, so with little confession one has received little forgiveness, and we find out that we love little. Forgiveness will produce love in our life, and love is Christ. Without confession of our sins, and without forgiving those who have wronged us, as it says in the Scripture, he who has confessed little, has been forgiven little, and loves little. Are you one who has forgiven much or forgiven little? The amount of love in our life is based on how much we forgive others and ask for forgiveness ourselves.

### 10.  Forgiveness is tied to the receiving of the Holy Spirit.

> Peter replied, "Repent and be baptized, every one of you, in the name of Jesus Christ for the forgiveness of your sins. And you will receive the gift of the Holy Spirit (Acts 2:38).

Hello? Forgiveness is tied to the receiving of the Holy Spirit, which means unforgiveness stops the receiving of the Holy Spirit.

This just drives me crazy! How much teaching is there on the Holy Spirit? There are thousands of books and teachings on "moving in the gifts of the Holy Spirit" and "receiving the Holy Spirit." This is so black and white. Repent, which means turn from your ways. It starts with confession and asking for forgiveness, or forgiving others. Be baptized and forgive in order to receive the Holy Spirit.

There is so much teaching on the Holy Spirit. Step one...step two.... Is forgiveness and confession anywhere in the process? No, but I can tell you there is a lot more religious nonsense attached to the process. Something as simple as confessing to receive forgiveness of your sins in the name of Jesus Christ and you *will*—not you might, or you'll get a part of it, or ten percent of the Holy Spirit—you *will* receive the gift of the Holy Spirit. It is a guarantee.

So repent, be baptized, confess, and forgive others, and you will receive forgiveness if you want the Holy Spirit in you and if you want to move in those gifts. Start confessing and forgiving. This is another reason why the devil works so hard on us to not forgive and confess— so we won't receive the Holy Spirit or the power that He brings into our lives. Instead, we are trying to play the "righteous and holy" part yet remain filled with wickedness. We all have "junk in our trunks," and it's time to clean it out.

## FORGIVENESS LEADS TO FREEDOM

Forgiveness shows up from Genesis through Revelation. It is one of the consistent threads throughout the Bible yet it is so little talked about or taught. We are commanded to forgive and to ask for forgiveness. We are commanded to get rid of anger, bitterness, malice, and resentment. Sin is tied to sickness, and forgiveness is tied to healing. We see leaders in the Bible who pray for their people and are willing for their own souls to go into hell so that others wouldn't go. Where is that kind of love demonstrated in the leadership of the Body of Christ today?

We see what provokes God to not forgive—and that is not forgiving each other. When we don't confess our sins to Him, as well as to each other, this provokes God not to forgive us. But God is provoked to forgive when we forgive one another. Walking in forgiveness brings the gift of the Holy Spirit. That's why it is so important to practice this as a way of life.

---

The fruit of forgiveness is freedom. So I challenge you, my brother or my sister, whether for selfish or noble reasons, to make a list right now of the people in the Body of Christ you need to forgive. Forgive every leader in the Body of Christ you've encountered who has been more concerned about their own success and about their building or programs rather than about how you are hurting. I truly believe that every leader in the Body of Christ has given it their best shot, but we've been trained in this culture to make the minor things in religion the major thing and we've made the major things of God the minor things, like forgiveness.

Every man, woman, or child who has ever slandered you, hurt you, lied about you, belittled you, stalked you, was jealous of you, judged you, misjudged you, told you to sit down and shut up—every man, woman, or child who molested you, violated you, or overlooked you for a promotion because of being intimidated by you, needs to be on that list. For everyone who did not encourage you, but instead spoke death over you, and everyone who wasn't there when you needed them—add them to the list.

This list should include those who have wronged you in the marketplace as well—every boss, non-Christian, manager, employee, associate. If they have misled you, ignored you, and purposely stayed away from you, now is the time to forgive them.

Your list needs to include a confession and forgiveness for yourself for every mistake and wrong thought. Be specific and root these things out of your heart.

Are you your worst critic? Do you daily have self-condemning thoughts in your mind? Are you constantly encouraging yourself to hide from these things that hold you back? If so, it's time to forgive yourself for all of those things that you are reminded of. And most importantly—forgive yourself for not forgiving those who hurt you and not asking God to forgive these people.

You may even need to forgive God. Maybe you have judged God. Maybe you felt like He wasn't there for you. Maybe you've blamed Him. Why did He allow certain things to happen to you? A lot of people have resentment toward God. Remove that bitterness toward Him by forgiving Him. I know this sounds crazy, but I promise you it works.

In our events, we go deeply into the root system that is within each person. We find that the root of unforgiveness is lying nearly dormant within everyone. And the proof is the bad fruit that continues to show up. The negative actions and annoying problems that seem to pop up in all of our lives can make living miserable. I can link every one of your hindering beliefs and fears to the root of unforgiveness. I can also link every negative feeling you have with people and personalities to the root of unforgiveness.

In fact, your beliefs about money, men, women, and God are all linked to something in your past. If these beliefs are negative, it's because of unforgiveness hiding deeply within you. Don't stay in that place of hindrance. Step up and do what many thousands of our clients have done—forgive. Repent from unforgiveness and bitterness and malice—all the things that I've talked about. Turn away now and allow the Lord to transform your heart and your mind. Allow Him to cleanse and purify you through and through. It is only then that I believe you can move forward into success in all areas of your life. Remember, your success is tied to your forgiveness.

## FORGIVENESS KILLED THE GIANT IN MY LIFE

My giant was unforgiveness. Situations like I've experienced are addressed on a very personal level in my monthly seminars. I help people walk through forgiveness, judgment, resentment, and bitterness concerning the failures and hindrances that may have been in their lives. In one session of our seminar, we deal with issues including abuse, business failures, molestation, tragedies, trauma, fears, abandonment, lack of motivation, self-confidence, procrastination, and over-stress they may have experienced. People cannot move forward unless they deal with the subject of forgiveness. So we attack it inside-out. Because I have walked through and have forgiven and I live in forgiveness, He has given me the authority to help others walk in freedom as well.

I had so many hang-ups about trusting. I couldn't trust or work with men *or* women. I found myself very defensive around people, always waiting for some disaster to happen. I found myself in multiple abusive situations with men and I was tired of it. My past of dealing with bad relationships with men nagged me, haunted me, and tormented me. I felt useless, worthless, and unlovable. I confessed this to the Lord.

I began forgiving the first man who I felt failed me and abused me—my stepfather. Once I had fully forgiven him I saw a vision of him being beaten with a broom by his mother. I began to weep and weep and weep and I had compassion for my stepdad who was taught how to be abusive by his "giant" mother.

After six years of absolute silence, my stepdad called me. He said, "I don't care if you ever want to see me again, and I don't blame you if you don't ever want your children to see me. I just want to let you know I'm proud of you."

That moment was worth all those 15 years of playing basketball and having him never show up to a game. That moment was worth him looking at a report card with straight As and a D and condemning the D. That was worth never doing anything right in his eyes. That was worth the constant belittling, put-downs, and name-calling. Hearing those words, "I'm proud of you," was worth it all!

Finally I was able to face my giant and leave standing!

To be clear, the giant in my life wasn't my giant stepfather. It was the giant issue of unforgiveness that led me down a path of self-destruction. That giant was the one that had to come down. Because of the bitterness and resentment that unforgiveness led to and all the judgments I had against people in authority and the men I encountered, once I tore down the giant of unforgiveness in my life I was then able to be in a functional relationship with my new husband, Hans (whom I met three months after my first husband stole everything). We have three sons who I am not emasculating—they are strong, young men. Our daughter Arika is submissive and honorable, a gorgeous, pure, and godly virgin who is very strong without being a little Jezebel like I was.

Obviously, I also had to forgive many Christians who had failed and hurt me. For starters, it was Brent, his parents, and the couple who adopted my daughter. God is so faithful to His Word, and because I forgave, He delivered my baby back into my arms, first when she was 14, and then she came to live with us full-time when she was 16. While Kristina lived with our family, I also walked her through forgiveness and taught her how to forgive, not only me and Brent and his parents, but also her adopted family. She now has a functional relationship with us, Brent and his family, *and* her adopted family. This truly is a miracle.

The point: If I hadn't forgiven the men in my life as well as the Christians who had deceived me, I certainly couldn't be speaking to Christians nor have men as clients. Without forgiveness, I would have been a feminist who hated Christians and spoke only to crowds of women. But that's not true. Over 50 percent of my clients are men and many of them have become my biggest supporters and promoters because of how their income has exploded and debt as been paid off. Some of the best success stories that have come out of our seminars have been from men; whether it's marriages that have been saved, debt being paid off, businesses exploding, or whatever.

The truth is, I speak to secular as well as Christian audiences, leading the unsaved to Christ and teaching those in Christ how to succeed in Christ. It could only happen because of the power of forgiveness that God has given us as a gracious gift. My past does not equal my current state of circumstances and neither does yours, unless you don't forgive.

So if you think that the individuals in your life who need your forgiveness are not forgivable, I can give you a long list of things that have been done to me that you would say are definitely unforgivable.

The truth is, I was held captive to unforgiveness. I am no longer. This giant has been killed, and it is time for you to slay yours.

Forgiveness has become a lifestyle for me because there will always be people who I will need to forgive. You will encounter them too. More people will be guilty of disappointing us, offending us, hurting us, stealing from us, attacking our character, and defrauding our reputations. It is possible that many of these may be our brothers and sisters in Christ, and even our spouses and children from time to time. But you have to make a choice to either walk in forgiveness and freedom or walk in unforgiveness, which leads to bitterness, resentment, hatred, malice, even depression, oppression, and suicide. Unforgiveness attacks your confidence. It demotivates you. It steals vision from you, and it also opens the door to sickness, death, and disease. It stops the flow of favor and prosperity from God in your life.

You have to make a conscious choice. It's either a lifestyle of forgiveness, which is forgiving people quickly to keep your heart and hands clean, or walk the path that the vast majority of people on this planet walk, which leads to death—a slow, tormented death. The choice is yours.

Please join me on this journey of Spirit-driven success and choose to do what a rare, peculiar breed of people will do—forgive.

### ENDNOTE

1.   Luke 15:4.

# CONCLUSION

At the beginning of this book, I asked whether you are satisfied financially, physically, mentally, emotionally, socially, relationally. My hope, my prayer, is that you now realize the skills and abilities, dormant within you, that are waiting to come out. These skills and abilities will increase satisfaction in every area of your life. You have the ability to do your heart's desire because God designed you for success. He did not intend for your life to be mediocre.

Please don't live your life condemned by your own excuses. Don't wait for the right circumstances because that time will never come. Please don't be like most defeated Christians waiting for things to happen and hoping to get lucky. Be the one He is looking for by getting out there and increasing your skills and abilities so that you are the right person for the next promotion. Do what Hans and I, as well as hundreds of thousands of our clients, have done. We have all learned specific skill sets that have massively changed our lives. These skill sets have enabled us to be unstoppable in the marketplace and victorious over the hand of the enemy.

I believe God is looking for people to step up and be equipped to succeed wildly in the marketplace for His Glory. You have read this message for a reason, and I believe it's because you are perhaps one of the many who will do what it takes to be a chosen vessel for such a time as this.

The world is desperate for real leadership right now. I have been so blessed to watch thousands of people get the equipping they needed so they could stop walking a path of mediocrity and start living a life of success in their finances, marriages, with their children, careers, and of expanding influence. They learned step by step how to succeed in those areas and applied what they learned, and God radically blessed the work of their hands.

If you do what they have done, He will bless you the same way. Come visit us sometime and see for yourself a breed of kings in the marketplace who are taking the Kingdom of God by storm and for His glory.

Don't wait until it's too late. Take *action!* Do something! The Spirit of the Living God is ready and willing to use you; are you ready? God truly does have a plan for your life. You have been anointed, set apart, and filled to overflowing with all of the tools and gifts that you need to accomplish that plan. And He who is in you is *able* to complete it!

Now you have a choice.

You can put down this book and go on living a mundane, predictable, mediocre, fearful life. Or you can respond to what you have just read and learn, like David, like Jesus, to go after your destiny! You must believe that you are who *He* clearly says you are. Believe that He is who He says He is. Then, in that confidence, move forward! Step out of the rut that you have been living in, the rut that you have been calling your life, and *rise up!*

## YOUR NEXT STEP

Reading is a good start, but if you want long-lasting results, you must put these principles of Spirit-driven success into action daily! My first suggestion is that you read this book from start to finish once a month for the next year. The little voice in your head might be saying, "Why do I need to read the book again and again?" The reason is that repetition is the mother of skill. The more you absorb the principles of Spirit-driven success, the faster you'll see results in your life as you become the person God designed you to be.

Over the years, I have had the honor and privilege of equipping hundreds of thousands—and growing daily—of people for success through my live seminars, tele-classes, audios, videos, and personal coaching and mentoring programs. Through these training programs, thousands have developed the skills to enrich their lives far beyond what they thought was possible.

The marketplace pays for value, and the way you increase your value to the market is by increasing your skill. This book is the beginning of a lifelong journey of a true relationship with God through Jesus Christ and His Holy Spirit *and* through ongoing development of your skills so that you can bring *value* to the marketplace and create impact for His Kingdom.

To help you increase your skill, I would like to give you a complimentary membership to one of our members-only training sites. Here you will have access to audio, video, and television programs and special reports valued at over $10,000 that will help you advance in all areas of your life, 24 hours a day 7 days a week.

As a member, you'll be equipped to develop your skill set so that you can compete head-to-head in the marketplace and succeed wildly for His glory. The training tools in our members sites will help you become a better business owner, marketer, executive, employee, salesperson, manager, parent, schoolteacher, community leader, or pastor. Whatever occupation, career, or business you are involved in, you'll find these free training resources invaluable.

To get instant access to these members-only tools, simply visit www.DaniJohnson.com right now and subscribe to one of our members-only sites.

Also, take advantage of my *special free CD offer!* For a limited time, we are offering a complimentary copy of "Conquering the Financial Kingdom." Inside this CD you will discover the seven traps that rob your prosperity, the ten laws of wealth, how the fruits of your choices show up in your finances, how God rewards your spirit of excellence, and a whole lot more.

Don't delay; head over to www.DaniJohnson.com right now and register as a complimentary RiseToSuccess.com or WorkAtHomeProfitZone.com member.

Dani Johnson is an author, speaker, trainer, and the founder of Call to Freedom International. She went from living out of her car with $2.03 to her name to earning her first million in two short years by the age of 23. Through her dynamic training seminars, many of her clients have become debt-free and have gone on to earn six- and seven-figure incomes.

Dani teaches and coaches with a passionate desire to see her clients become transformed in their spiritual, family, and professional lives. Her clients become warriors in the marketplace, demonstrating God's glory in places where the Church cannot reach.

In addition to Bible revelation, her seminars offer step-by-step strategies on business development, wealth development, debt annihilation, conflict resolution, powerful sales and marketing training, management skills, growth skills, team building skill, people development and leadership development skills, time management skills, marriage and parenting skills, extremely powerful communication skills, as well as spiritual equipping.

Clients range from rocket scientists to home schooling moms. She has personally consulted and coached members from a wide range of professions, including doctors, lawyers, judges, scientists, seismologists, actors, film directors, politicians, large- and small-business leaders, all types of salespersons, restaurant servers, mechanics, construction workers and contractors, hair salon owners, spa owners, pilots, flight attendants, bankers, branch managers, financial planners and investors, real estate agents, brokers, pastors, missionaries, musicians, artists, elders, singers, songwriters, and even opera singers.

Dani's passion is helping people break through barriers that stop them from experiencing true freedom emotionally, mentally, spiritually, and financially.

## A SPECIAL NOTE FROM DANI

Has *Spirit-Driven Success* impacted your life? Has it made a difference in how you see yourself, how you see God, and how you see your part in building His Kingdom? Do you plan to use the principles revealed in *Spirit-Driven Success* to enrich your life spiritually and financially? Do you plan to use these principles to get a promotion or a raise at work, to start a new business, or to take an existing business from struggling or failing to exponential growth and success? Will you use *Spirit-Driven Success* to become debt-free and wealthy so that you can be that light on a hill that the world will see so that your Father in Heaven may be glorified (see Matt. 5:14)?

If so, will you help me help others? Will you help me share the message of *Spirit-Driven Success* with the rest of the world? If *Spirit-Driven Success* has impacted you, if it has changed your life and set you free, think of those you know who you would like to share this gift with. I am asking for your help. Millions of Christians and non-Christians alike are in bondage like I was. This message changed my life, and it has now changed the life of tens of thousands of others for His glory. I want to see it spread across the world because I know what my life would be today had I not received and acted on the principles in this book—I don't even want to think about it.

Will you help me spread this message? I can't do it alone. You can make a huge difference. Will you? If so, please consider the following ideas:

1.   Make a list of names, of people you want to bless with *Spirit-Driven Success*. Who do you know who has influence (pastor, community leader, board member, CEO, or executive)? Who do you know in your church, school, or workplace? Who do you know who is a business owner or marketer? Who do you know who is struggling to make ends meet and needs a promotion at their job? Who do you know who doesn't yet know their true purpose in life? Who do you know in your family who needs to experience healing emotionally, mentally, and spiritually?

2   Use your list:

    a.   Call them right now and tell them about *Spirit-Driven Success*. Tell them how it's impacted you, and share your story. Give them our Web site (www.DaniJohnson.com or www.SpiritDrivenSuccess.com) where they can get their very own copy, shipped out to them within 24 hours.

    b.   Go to our Web site and order multiple copies of the book as a gift. You can have the book shipped directly to your friends, business associates, or family members as a gift from you. Discounts are available for bulk orders.

    c.   Go to www.SpiritDrivenSuccess.com and use our refer-a-friend feature to send an e-mail invitation to your contacts to visit our Web site and get more info about *Spirit-Driven Success*. You can use this tool to import your entire address book or contact list to receive a message from you (sent from our servers) about *Spirit-Driven Success*.

# OTHER TRAINING FROM DANI JOHNSON

### IS AVAILABLE AT
### WWW.DANIJOHNSON.COM

*Uncovering the Mysteries of Success*
Live Audio Training Series

*Spirit-Driven Success*
Live Audio Training Series

*Christian-Based Training*
Live Audio Training

*War on Debt*
Home Study Course

*Grooming the Next Generation for Success*
Home Study Course

Free Monthly Training Call

We'll also give you a complimentary membership to our members-only site, where you'll get access to exclusive Dani Johnson audio and video content to help you experience more *Spirit-Driven Success* in your life!

Go ahead, do it now!

**www.DaniJohnson.com/freecfkcd**

# FREE MP3 DOWNLOAD!!

HURRY! Download Dani Johnson's
**"Conquering the Financial Kingdom"** MP3 **FREE!**

Learn and conquer the seven habits that lead to poverty and financial struggle. You'll also discover the ten steps to create wealth, prosperity, and success in your life, and much more!

Just visit: www.SpiritDrivenSuccess.com/freedownload.

**We'll also give you updates from
Dani Johnson about *Spirit-Driven Success!***

Additional copies of this book and other
book titles from DESTINY IMAGE are
available at your local bookstore.

Call toll-free: 1-800-722-6774.

Send a request for a catalog to:

**Destiny Image® Publishers, Inc.**
P.O. Box 310
Shippensburg, PA 17257-0310

*"Speaking to the Purposes of God for This
Generation and for the Generations to Come."*

**For a complete list of our titles,
visit us at www.destinyimage.com.**